Willis Boyd Allen

Silver rags

Willis Boyd Allen

Silver rags

ISBN/EAN: 9783743323216

Manufactured in Europe, USA, Canada, Australia, Japa

Cover: Foto ©ninafisch / pixelio.de

Manufactured and distributed by brebook publishing software (www.brebook.com)

Willis Boyd Allen

Silver rags

SILVER RAGS

BY

WILLIS BOYD ALLEN

Author of "PINE CONES"

"Like beggared princes of the wood,
In silver rags the birches stood."

BOSTON
LOTHROP PUBLISHING COMPANY

COPYRIGHT, 1886,
BY
WILLIS BOYD ALLEN

TO
THE LITTLE PRINCESS
ISADORE

CONTENTS.

Chapter		Page
I.	Overboard!	7
II.	Where is the Watch?	21
III.	The Trial	41
IV.	Fire!	52
V.	In the Den	74
VI.	A Small Hero	92
VII.	Oak Leaves and Hay	110
VIII.	Poor Tom!	129
IX.	A Mountain Camp	137
X.	The Storm	158
XI.	The Great Base-Ball Match	172
XII.	Hunted to Earth	185
XIII.	Found at Last	196
XIV.	Quiet Days at The Pines	207
XV.	Good-bye!	216

SILVER RAGS.

CHAPTER I.

OVERBOARD.

"HELP! Help!"

It was a girl's voice, clear and sharp with distress. The cry echoed over Loon Pond, and rang through the woods which surrounded its dimpled waters.

In a small, flat-bottomed boat, about fifty yards from the shore, crouched a young girl of perhaps sixteen years, her face blanched with terror as she gazed into the depths beneath and uttered again and again that piercing cry:

"Help! O quick, quick! Help!"

Something dark rose slowly to the surface of the pond, and a small white hand waved frantically in the air a moment, then sank, struggling, out of sight. Again it came up, this time more quietly, and again disappeared, while the occupant of the boat screamed louder, her voice breaking into sobs. The only oar to be seen was floating quietly on the water, almost within reach.

"Help!"

Would no one come? The birches that crowned the hill-top close by shivered in the sunlight; on the farther shore, the pines stood motionless in dark, silent ranks.

Just as the object in the water rose for the third and last time, scarcely breaking the surface, the bushes hiding the nearest bank suddenly parted, and a boy dashed out into the pond which was shallow at this point, with a smooth, sandy beach.

"Hold on, Kittie, I'm coming!" he shouted lustily, splashing ahead with all his might, and making the water fly in every direction.

Presently he sank deeper, and began to swim with such powerful strokes that half a dozen of them brought him nearly alongside the boat.

"There, there, Randolph!" screamed Kittie Percival, pointing to the sinking form.

Randolph gave one look, doubled over in the water, and with a desperate effort dived headlong in a line to cut off the drowning girl before she reached the bottom. After a few seconds which to Kittie seemed days, he reappeared, holding his helpless burden, and clutched the stern of the boat. The poor girl's head lay back on his shoulder, white, cold, and motionless.

"Haven't — you — got — an oar?" puffed Randolph.

"It fell out when I wasn't noticing," sobbed Kittie, "and floated off. We both leaned over to reach it, and Pet fell into the pond."

"All right, I'll swim for it. Here goes." And allowing his feet to rise behind him, with one arm around the girl and the other hand still grasping the boat, he struck out, frog-fashion, for the shore. Presently he resumed his upright position, but found the water was still over his head. A dozen more pushes, and the second experiment was successful. He announced that he felt bottom under his feet, and presently the bow of the boat grated on the sand. Kittie now jumped into the water beside him, regardless of skirts and boots, and assisted him in raising the unconscious girl, from whose garments and long, bright hair the water streamed as they lifted her tenderly in their arms, and carried her to the shore.

While they were thus engaged, a third actor appeared on the scene, no other than "Captain Bess" Percival herself, whom, with her sister Kittie, the readers of *Pine Cones* will remember.

"O Kittie, Kittie, what has happened? Did she fall overboard? Is she alive?"

"We don't know," panted Randolph, answering her last question. "She was just going down the third time. Where shall we take her?"

"Up to the Indians' tent," said Bess. "It's only a few steps from here. I left Tom and Ruel there, while I came to look for you. Here, let me help."

"Bring her lilies," added Kittie sadly. "Poor little Pet, she had only gathered two!"

The mournful procession took up its march through the woods, Bess and Randolph carrying Pet between them. Kittie followed, with the lilies, helping when she could.

Pet Sibley was a girl slightly younger than her companions, who lived near the Percivals in Boston. When the invitation came from uncle Will Percival in June for them to spend their summer vacation, or a part of it, with him and aunt Puss — as the children called his wife — at The Pines, the girls begged permission, which was heartily granted, to bring their friend Pet with them. She was a frank, good-hearted girl, with light, rippling hair, blue eyes, and a sunny disposition which always looked on the bright side of everything and perhaps was a bit too forgetful of the earnest in life. If that, and her evident pleasure in her own pretty face, were faults, they were very forgivable ones; for she was sweet and true at heart, after all. The fun of the whole thing was, that she had never lived in the country. She was a thoroughly city-bred girl; had travelled in Europe when she was a wee child, had lived two or three years in hotels and "apartments," and knew absolutely nothing of field and forest. A more complete contrast to sober, thoughtful Kittie, and energetic "Captain Bess," could hardly be imagined. So it came about that, as often happens with people of widely varying dispositions, all three loved one another dearly.

Randolph was in the second class at the Boston Latin School, and had won three prizes that spring, two for scholarship, and one for drilling.

On this particular morning Ruel, a guide, trapper, and man-of-all-work at Mr. Percival's farm in the heart of the Maine woods, had taken the young folks off for a tramp to Loon Pond, a pretty sheet of water some four miles long by one and a half broad. They had enjoyed themselves immensely — Randolph, Tom, and the three girls — running races along the forest paths, gathering mosses, ferns and queer white "Indian pipes," or listening to Ruel's quaint sayings as he talked of birds and wild creatures of the wood, with not a little philosophy thrown in.

At the distance of about a furlong from the pond, they had come out upon a little clearing, on the further edge of which was a rude tent of canvas. In the doorway sat an Indian squaw, with one tiny brown pappoose in her arms, and another playing on the grass near by. The father of the babies she said, on inquiry, was off somewhere in the woods. She had a few baskets for sale, and while Bess and the two boys stopped to look at these and play with the babies, Kittie and Pet had run on ahead, and having reached the shore of the pond, had come upon an old boat, apparently used for a long time past by no one, except perhaps the Indian when he was not too lazy to fish. Into this boat they had climbed, screaming and laughing, girl-fashion, and hastily pushing it off with the one oar which lay in the bottom, had been trying to collect a bunch of lilies to surprise the rest, when the accident happened as Kittie described it.

It took but a few minutes for the mournful little group to reach the camp, though the distance seemed miles. Pet showed not the slightest sign of life and her pretty hair almost touched the ground as it hung over Randolph's shoulder and swayed to and fro as he walked.

Ruel's quick eye was the first to catch sight of them, and to take in the situation.

"Bring her here," he said sharply, springing to his feet and wasting no time in questions. "Now turn her on her face — so — there, that'll do. Poor little gal! I dunno whether we c'n bring her to, but we c'n try, anyhow."

"Shall I run for the doctor, Ruel?" asked Tom, trembling from head to foot.

"No doctor nearer'n six mile," said the guide grimly. "By the time he'd git here we shouldn't need him, either ways. Bess, you'n' Kittie take her inside the tent — here, let me lift her — git her wet clothes off an' roll her in blankets. Grab 'em up anywhere you c'n find 'em. I'll fix it with the Injuns. Randolph, you're wet's a mink yourself. Take Tom with you and run fer home. Mis'

Percival will give ye some hot tea and put ye to bed."

"But what shall I do, Ruel?" asked Tom again.

"You git a couple of them big gray shawls of your aunt's an' bring 'em in the double team to the back road, where this path comes out — remember it?"

"Yes, Ruel, but —"

"Git Tim to put the horses in, and drive. He'll hurry 'nuff, once git him goin'."

Tom and Randolph were off like a flash, and Ruel turned to the squaw, who had been standing motionless, after having picked up her pappoose that Ruel had tipped over when he jumped up.

"Say, Moll, can't ye take holt and help the gals a little?"

The squaw came forward crossly enough, mumbling and grumbling to herself, and, entering the tent, pulled the flap down behind her. Once inside, she worked harder than any of them, with hands as gentle and skilful as those of a hospital nurse.

Fifteen minutes passed. It was a hot day in late June, and Ruel wiped his brow repeatedly as he paced to and fro before the tent. The Indian, he knew, would bear no interference, and her knowledge and experience were invaluable.

"Any signs of life?" he asked aloud, when he could bear the suspense no longer.

Kittie put a white face out between the hangings, and said "No."

Twenty minutes. A thrush from a thicket near by, sang a few notes, and stopped. The air went up in little waves of heat, from the tree-tops. It was very still.

Suddenly there was an exclamation inside the tent; both girls cried out at once, and were hushed by the guttural tones of the Indian.

Another long silence, almost unendurable to the big-hearted man outside, who felt in some way accountable for what had happened.

He hid his face in his hands, and walked slowly off toward the thicket where the thrush had sung.

Again there was a stir within the tent.

"See!" cried Bess joyfully. "She moved her eyelids! She's alive! She's alive!"

Soon a new voice was heard behind the canvas — a low, troubled moan, then a pitiful crying, like that of a beaten child. Poor little Pet, it was hard, coming back to life again! She writhed in agony for a few minutes, crying and catching her breath brokenly. But at last her sweet blue eyes opened. "Mamma!" she said, with trembling lips, looking about wonderingly at her strange surroundings.

"O Pet, darling, I'm so glad!" sobbed Kittie, falling on her knees and kissing the pale face again and again. "You're all safe and alive! It was my fault, taking you out — of course you thought it was like the Public Gardens — oh, dear, and here are your two lilies!" And Kittie burst out crying afresh at sight of them.

While she had been talking, Pet had gazed at her and the dark face of the Indian alternately. Slowly came back the memory of the walk in the woods, the first view of the shining lake, the laughing scramble into the boat, the fair lily faces, looking up at her. Then, the terrible moment when she felt herself falling down, down, with all the the world flying away from her, and only the thick, green, stifling water pressing against her face.

She tried to put up her little hands to shut out the picture, but she was too tightly rolled in the blanket. Then she looked up and — laughed! At the same moment the Indian threw back the tent-flap, and beckoned to Ruel, who was hurrying toward her at the sound of the voices. Pet lay swathed in cloths and blankets of all colors, as old Moll had snatched them from bed and floor, so that up to her chin she looked like a gay-colored little mummy. Her head, with its long golden hair, rested in Bessie's lap; and a smile was on her lips.

"Thank God!" exclaimed Ruel, taking off his woodsman's cap. Then he dropped into his old-fashioned, easy drawl once more, and commenced active preparations for the homeward trip.

"I — think I — can — walk —" whispered Pet faintly, wriggling a little in her cocoon.

"Wall, I've no doubt you c'd fly, ef we'd let ye," remarked the guide, busying himself in wringing out her wet clothes and rolling them into a bundle; "but I guess we'll hev the fun of carryin' of ye, this time. Tom'll be back soon —"

"Here he comes, now!" interrupted Bess, as the boy hurried forward with his arms full of shawls.

"Is she — is she — ?" he stammered, halting a few paces distant.

"She's all right, my boy," said Ruel kindly. "She's ben a laughin', and is all high fer walkin' home, ef we'd let her."

The boy's face twitched with emotion, and in spite of himself he could not prevent two or three tears from rolling over his cheeks.

"Here's some cordial," he managed to say, "that aunt Puss said would — would be good for her. And uncle Will himself was at home, and will meet us at the cross-road with his team."

Before leaving the tent, Ruel, at Tom's request, tried to make Moll accept a small sum for her services. But she would not take a cent.

"These Injuns are queer people," said Ruel, leading the way with Pet in his arms, toward the road. "Sometimes they do act like angels from heaven, an' sometimes — they don't! You never know whar to hev 'em."

"Where does this family come from?" asked Tom, trudging beside Ruel and holding twigs aside from Pet's face.

"From up North somewhars. They won't tell who they are, and I shall be glad, fer one, when they leave."

"I shall be thankful to them as long as I live, for what that woman did for Pet," said Kittie warmly.

"Wall, that's so; she was a master hand, an'

no mistake. Give me an Injun fer any kind of a hurt you kin git in the woods."

Right glad were they all to find uncle Will and his noble grays, waiting for them at the road. Just what the kind old man had suffered, sitting there helplessly for the last five minutes, no one will ever know — except perhaps his gentle wife Eunice — "aunt Puss" — with whom he talked the whole matter over, after the children had gone to bed that night.

In a moment he had Pet in his trembling arms, and with Ruel at the reins they were all soon comfortably disposed in the big wagon, and rattling homeward.

How they drove up to the door of the farm-house, with Pet waving her slender white hand feebly, between Bess and Kittie; how aunt Puss, strong woman as she was, broke down utterly at sight of her, and afterward hugged her, and cried over her, and "cosseted" her, the rest of that memorable day, need not be described. Enough to say that Pet steadily regained her strength, and by night was able to sit with the rest under the broad elms before the house and listen to uncle Percival's stories.

It was not until bed time that as the girls were going slowly up-stairs, arm in arm, she stopped suddenly, and exclaimed "My watch!"

"Your watch?" echoed the others. "Why, what's the matter with it?"

"It's lost!"

"Lost?"

"I wore it to the pond this morning. It was that lovely little watch that mamma gave me last Christmas, gold and blue enamel, with my name in it. There was a chain, too, and a tiny key. Oh, dear, what shall I do! Where can it be? It couldn't have fallen out, for 'twas hooked into my button-hole, just as tight!"

"I can tell you what's become of your watch, Pet," exclaimed Randolph, from the hall below.

"What?"

"The Indians!"

CHAPTER II.

WHERE IS THE WATCH?

"I'M afraid," said Mr. Percival at breakfast next morning, "that your watch will not be recovered, Pet. I sent Ruel over to the pond two hours ago, and he reports that the Indians are gone, bag and baggage. They generally stay only a few weeks at a time in any one spot."

"I thought I saw a queer look in old Moll's face when we left," put in Ruel, joining the conversation with a down-East "hired-man's" freedom. "You know she wouldn't take any money, which, with an Injun, is 'nuff to make you suspect somethin's up."

Tom was sleeping late, and had not come down to breakfast. At The Pines, one of the comforts was that you could sleep just as long as you wanted to in the morning.

"They're growing young things," aunt Puss would say, "and they have to get up early all winter to get ready for school. It's a pity if they can't lie abed here, so long's they're resting, till afternoon, if they like."

The real fact was that ordinarily the days were so filled with good times that noboby wished to lose an hour in the morning, and so all hands were up bright and early.

"How much do you think the watch was worth, Pet?" asked her aunt. "Bessie, let me give you another mug of milk."

Pet sat next to aunt Puss, looking very pale and quiet this morning. It was observed that she started nervously every time she was addressed; but this remnant of yesterday's fright wore off during the day.

"I don't know exactly," she answered, "but I think mamma paid six hundred francs for it in Geneva last year."

"That's about one hundred and twenty dollars," said Mr. Percival. "It would be worth at least a hundred and fifty in America, when it was new."

"Can't it have dropped out of her pocket?" suggested Kittie.

"Ruel searched every foot of ground where you went."

"Why can't the thieves be pursued?" exclaimed Randolph, starting to his feet. "I'll join a party, for one, to overtake them and recover the property!"

"Sit down and finish your coffee, my boy," said his uncle, smiling. "The sheriff and two assistants started on their track half an hour ago. But I fear it won't be of much use, as they are too cunning to be easily caught. Of course they will deny all knowledge of the watch, probably having hidden it when they heard the officers coming."

"Will they be arrested?"

"Yes."

The girls began to look frightened.

"And where will they be brought, sir?"

"Here. I am a Trial Justice in this county," said Mr. Percival, rising.

Just then Tom entered the room, looking as if he had not slept very soundly, after all.

"Uncle," he said in a low voice, glancing at the rest as they left their places at the table with a clatter of chairs on the kitchen floor, "uncle, can I see you alone for a moment?"

Mr. Percival patted him on the shoulder. "Better eat your breakfast, my boy, the first thing you do. I have some matters to look after in the barn and you can find me there, if you want to. You must forget about the accident yesterday," he added kindly, seeing the boy's pale face. "Pet's all right now, and we sha'n't let her fall in again, you may be sure."

"I know, sir, but —"

Here aunt Puss bustled up with a plate of hot flapjacks, and uncle Will stepped aside with a laugh.

"Eat 'em while they're hot, Tom," said Ruel gravely, pausing a minute at the door, "or Mis' Percival will have her feelin's awfully hurt."

So Tom was fain to put off his interview with his uncle, till some better season. Ah, Tom, if you had but spoken a moment earlier, or insisted one whit more strongly! But Mr. Percival went off where his duties called him, and Tom found no chance to see him alone that day, nor the next. Whatever the subject was, it did not seem to disturb him so much after a good breakfast; and he promised himself he would attend to it a little later.

The forenoon was spent quietly in the barn, in the capacious bays of which the mounds of fragrant hay had just been stored, still warm with the midsummer sunshine, and furnishing an occasional sleepy grasshopper, by no means startled out of his dignity by his sudden change of residence. The west wind blew softly in at the open doors, through which one could look, as one lay on the mow, into the sunny world outside, and catch a few bars of an oriole's call, or of robin's cheery note. The cattle were all out to pasture. Over the floor walked the hens, in serene meditation, placidly clucking, or uttering a remonstrative and warning "Wha-a-a-t!" as a swallow careened too near them in the bars of dusty sunlight. The only other noise was the occasional bird-twitter from one of the dozen or more nests upon the rafters overhead, and the tapping of bills on the floor as the sober fowls now and then gleaned a stray insect or bit of seed-food.

"I don't see," said Tom lazily, gazing up toward the ridge-pole, where a swallow was busily engaged in feeding her clamorous family, " I don't see what people ever want to live in the city for!"

"If people could spend their time on hay-mows, half asleep, or — Ow! — tickling their sisters' ears with straws! — "

"Well, that's all girls do, anyway. A feller might just's well stretch out here as curl up on a sofa and *crochet* all day!" Tom delivered this remark with emphasis, expressive of his manly disgust at all fancy-work in general, and "crochet" under which head he classed every home industry connected with worsted — in particular.

"I should like to see a 'feller' do Kensington," remarked Bess calmly. "Seems to me I remember one who wanted to knit on a spool, one time when he was sick, and —"

"O let up, Bess; that don't count?"

"— And after he had knit two inches and dropped thirteen stitches, gave it up because 'it made his head tired!'" concluded Bess mercilessly.

When the laugh had subsided, and Bess had emerged from the armful of dried clover and redtop under which Tom had extinguished her, Kittie spoke up, more soberly.

"I guess I know what Tom means, and he isn't so far out of the way either. We do waste lots of time now, really, don't we, girls?"

"So do boys," said Bess, stoutly.

"I know; but boys have something hard and

useful to do, 'most every day," persisted Kittie, whom the five Justices of the Supreme Bench couldn't have diverted from her point. "Boys go to school until they're ready to work or enter college. Then they never stop working, till they die."

"Yes," said Tom solemnly, "that's what uses me up so; it's just hard work."

"You look like it!" exclaimed Randolph, burying Tom in his turn. "I'll tell you what it is, girls," he added, as he gave Tom a final shot, "there's a good deal in what Kittie says. But work is good for us, anyway; and besides, when we do get in a little play, betweenwhiles, we have a glorious time, I can tell you!"

"But I know lots of boys, and young men too," put in Pet eagerly, "who just go to parties and don't work hard at all."

"O, I don't count those things *boys*," said Kittie. "They're just dolls; and if there's anything I always despised, it's boy-dolls."

"What do you think girls could do, Kittie?" asked Bess, "when they don't have lessons to get, I mean."

"I think they could make useful things to give

poor people," answered Kittie, her gray eyes sparkling with earnestness. "If we put the same amount of time into making up nice, plain clothes for poor people — special poor people, I mean, that we could find out about, ourselves — that we do into 'crochet,' as Tom says — what a lot of things we could make and give away in one winter!"

"I never could bear to sew," sighed Pet, surveying her pretty, plump fingers. "It seems just old ladies' work, pulling over rag-bags and 'piecing' together. It's dreadful, trying to save."

"It depends on what you do with the rags," said Randolph. "My grandmother had one of those bags that she was always using out of, and yet 'twas always full of rags, just crammed, so you couldn't pull the puckers of the bag together at the top."

"What ever did she make with them?"

"Mats and carpets, mostly. That is, she didn't make 'em herself, but used to hire poor people to make 'em, after she'd showed them how. She'd always arrange it so's to help two at once. 'It's better,' she used to say, 'to fe   with one crumb, than kill them with

"Why, how did she do it?" queried practical Bess, much interested.

"She'd find out through the city missionaries generally, some woman that was awfully poor, and she'd send for her and say, 'I know a family down in such a street that are very poor; they earn just enough to live on — not enough to *walk* on, for they haven't any carpets on their bare floors, this cold weather.'"

"Well?"

"Well, then she'd show the poor woman, the first one, how to 'pull' a rag mat, and would hire her to make one, giving her enough rags from that bag. When 'twas done, she'd praise it up and say how pretty 'twas, 'specially this row, or that flower, and so on; and then pay her for the work."

"And did your grandmother give the first poor woman's carpet to the second poor woman?" asked Pet, knitting her brows over the algebraic difficulty of the problem.

"Not herself. She sent it by the first poor woman so's to let her have the pleasure of giving."

"How lovely!" exclaimed Pet. "I'm going to

have a rag-bag of my very own this winter — with nothing but plush in it!"

"No," said Bess, "that won't do; plush catches dust."

"Who's up in my hay-mow!" The voice was deep and strong, but entirely pleasant, and so nearly underneath them that the girls jumped.

"O uncle Will, they all cried at once," do come up here — it's just perfect — and tell us a story!"

"If it's 'just perfect' already, I don't think I'd better come!" Nevertheless the good-natured old man mounted the steep ladder, and was at once allotted the breeziest and softest seat.

"Well, well," he said, baring his head to the gentle west wind, "this is comfortable. How many times I've lain on the hay here, when I was a boy, and dreamed what I would do — sometime!"

"You never dreamed yourself such a dear uncle as you are," said Bess softly, stroking his hair.

"Now you are trying to spoil me! What story shall I tell, I wonder? It must be short, because I may be called away at any moment. Let me see — how would one of my younger day scrapes do?"

"Splendid! splendid!"

"Well, this wasn't much of an adventure for youngsters like you who travel about over the country, a hundred miles a day. But to us, Fred and me, it seemed a good deal at the time. Fred always loved mountain climbing. He went to Europe while still a young man, and only last week he sent me a paper containing an account of his ascent of one of the loftiest among the Bernese Alps."

"Is he the stout gentleman that we saw here last summer, uncle, and who told us so much about Switzerland?"

"The same one, Kittie. 'Frederic Cruden, Esq , F. R. S.,' he is now. But in those days he was just a slim, fun-loving boy, and the only 'Fellow' he was, was a very good fellow indeed. Well, while we were both in our teens, our two families made up a party and visited the White Mountains."

"There was no railroad through the Notch then?"

"I should say not! If one wished to see the grandest localities of the White Mountains, he must either foot it or ride over the rough roads in the big, jolting stage-coach which often carried more outside than in, and occasionally tipped its passengers out upon the moss-banks beside the road. Bears, too, were more abundant than now, and that's saying considerable; for in many of the little New Hampshire towns of Coos County, farmers are to-day prevented from keeping sheep by the inroads of Bruin, who loves a dainty shoulder of mutton for supper only too well. I saw by the papers recently that the selectmen of one township during last year paid bounties on eleven bears and two wolves!"

Here Tom uttered a series of ferocious growls, but was covered with hay and sat upon by his cousin until he promised to behave himself.

"We were stopping at the fine, new Profile House," continued Mr. Percival, "Fred and I, with our fathers and mothers, as I said. Being of nearly the same age, we were always planning some sort of excursion together. One day we had begged to be allowed to ascend Mount Lafayette, a peak about twenty miles southwest of Mount Washington, and only second to the latter in point of interest. A guide-book which we had procured told of a fine house on the summit, and we would just stop there long enough to cool off after our walk, before coming down by the 'well-worn bridle-path.' We were sturdy little fellows, and though we had never yet accomplished such a feat as the ascent of a five thousand-foot mountain, felt quite equal to the task."

"How old did you say you were, uncle?" asked Randolph.

"About fourteen, but large of our age. We started off at about two o'clock in the afternoon, with many injunctions to be back by tea-time, and on no account to linger by the way.

"It was in the highest of spirits that we strode away on the level road, up the valley, toward the peak that lay so softly brown against the blue sky just beyond. Before long we struck into the bridle path, which was exceedingly muddy near the base, and became constantly more steep and slippery as we ascended. Boy-like, we were quite heedless of the lapse of time, and often stopped to gather birch-bark, climb after squirrels' nests, or take a bite of the sandwiches we had stuffed into our pockets at the last moment. The forest, I remember, was singularly silent, no breeze among the stiff tops of the hemlocks, no merry singing of birds; only now and then the muffled gurgle of a brook among the mossy stones beside the path, or the single, plaintive whistle of a thrush, far away on the mountain-side.

"When we had stopped for breath, about half-way up, a descending horseback-party passed us. We asked them about the house on the summit, but they only laughed, and said it had good walls and a high roof. This disturbed us a little, but we soon forgot our apprehensions, and pressed forward. Half a mile beyond this point, we came to that strange, nameless pool of water, seeming half cloud, half dream, hanging like a dew-drop on the slope of the mountain. As we stamped our feet on the moss which composed its banks, the whole surface of the ground, for rods away, trembled as if with an earthquake, and made us feel as if we were walking in a nightmare. It occurred to us that it would add to the glory of our exploit if we could catch some dream-fish out of this strange, unreal pond among the clouds; so we spent an hour or more in useless angling in its clear depths.

"Then Fred looked up at the sky, and uttered an exclamation. I followed his glance — and dropped my pole. The sun was almost resting on the edge of the mountains in the west, and it was plain that it would be dark in less than an hour."

"And all those bears!" murmured Pet, gazing at the narrator with round eyes. "O, I should think you *would* have been scared!"

Mr. Percival smiled. "If I had been as old as I am now, I should have said 'Fred, we're caught this time by our own thoughtlessness. We can go down in half or quarter of the time it took us to climb up; and once on the main road in the valley, we shall be all right.' But a boy of fourteen doesn't reason in that way. We were tired and hungry. We thought of the welcome we should receive from the people on the summit, and of the good things they would doubtless have for supper.

"'Besides,' said Fred, 'we must be nearly up now. The trees don't last much longer — they aren't higher than our heads here. It'll be all rocks pretty soon, and then we shall be right at the top, just like Mt. Washington.'

"So we started up again, with, we afterward confessed to each other, uncomfortable misgivings in our breasts. It was really my fault, though, for I was the older of the two, and ought to have known better.

"Well, in ten minutes the sun was out of sight behind the hills, and I tell you, boys, the shadows felt cold. It was like walking into a running brook in the middle of a hot day, and we shivered and buttoned our jackets tight around our throats as we clambered along over the rocks, panting in the thin air, and stopping for breath every few rods.

"It was tough work, especially as the wind began to rise and dodge at us from behind great bowlders, cutting like knives with its chilling breath. Darker and darker it grew, so that we could hardly distinguish the path, that was now a mere series of scratches over the rocks. In vain we strained our eyes for a friendly twinkle of light from the windows ahead. All was still, silent, dark. I confess, Pet, I thought of the bears, and halted half a dozen times, with beating heart, at sight of some dark rock that crouched behind the path. We were just thinking, Fred and I, of curling up for shelter under some overhanging ledge, and so spending the night, when a queer object caught our eyes. It was like a tree, stripped of every branch, and standing grimly alone there in the rocky desert, like a solitary Arab. A few steps more showed us what it was, and, at the same time, the tremendous mistake we had made, from the very outset of our plan, flashed upon us. It was clear that we were at last standing upon the very tip-top of Mount Lafayette, lifted in the air nearly a mile straight up, above the level of our home by the seashore. But alas, where was the inn, with its longed-for fires, its well-spread table, its comfortable beds and friendly hosts? The little weather-beaten flag-pole (for such was our naked tree), stood stiffly erect beside a blackened and crumbling stone wall, which enclosed a small space partially floored with charred boards, partially choked with rubbish that had fallen in long ago.

"'Seems to me I remember something about its being burned up once,' said Fred, faintly. 'I s'posed of course they built it again!'

"Yes, there were the openings, where windows and door had been set, and which now looked out into the dreary night like eyeless sockets.

"There was no time to be lost. The air was growing colder every moment, and the bitter wind was driving up a huge bank of clouds from the east. Although it was early in September, we afterward learned that ice formed in many places through the mountains that night. Such cases are by no means rare, and, indeed, in some of the ravines and gorges of the White Mountain group, snow and ice may be found the whole year round.

"Entering the roofless walls, and placing our sandwiches in a small niche which probably had once served for a cupboard, we set vigorously to work, ripping up the pieces of boards that still remained, and piling them in one corner where the wall was highest. In five minutes we had a roaring fire, by the light and warmth of which we constructed a rude shelter in the form of a 'lean-to,' against the rocks, and crept under it to sup off our scanty provisions, and reflect."

"Were you frightened, sir?" asked Tom slyly.

"Well, I suppose there was no great danger, Tom, but to boys who had spent their lives in comfortable homes, surrounded by care, and gentle, watchful attentions from those they loved most, it was a thrilling experience. There, alone on the mountain-top, high in air, far above any trace of vegetation save a few frightened Alpine flowers that huddle together under the rocks for a few weeks in summer, the darkness about them like a shroud, the wind rising and moaning over the bare ledges, and a storm creeping up through the valleys to assault their fortress at any moment. At last it came. Like a tornado, an icy blast rushed upon us with a howl and a roar, blowing our fire out in a moment while the red flames leaped back to the glowing brands only to be hurled off into the darkness again and again.

"And the rain! In less time than it takes to tell it, we were drenched to the skin, and pinched and pulled by the fingers of the storm that were thrust in through a hundred little crannies in our almost useless shelter. The thunder crashed, the rain rattled on the loose boards, the fire hissed feebly and turned black in the face, and the night closed in about us colder and drearier than ever. All we could do was to lie still, and shiver, and hope for morning.

"A little after midnight the tempest abated, and, tired, healthy boys as we were, we dropped into a troubled sleep. At the first glimmer of daylight, however, we stretched ourselves with groans and moans, and crawled stiffly out into the open air. It was bitter, bitter cold; so that I remember it was a long while before I could manage my fingers well enough to light a match.

"What did we do for kindling? Why, I forgot to

say that when it first began to rain, I took out all the birch bark I had gathered on my way up, and tucked it under my shoulder; so that for the most part the inner strips were pretty dry, and sputtered cheerily when I touched them off. I believe nothing ever did me so much good as that fire. Under its influence, we were so much cheered that we actually walked out to see the sunrise, which was glorious.

"It didn't take us long to descend that mountain, I can tell you; and we reached the Profile House in season to tell the whole story to the family (who, in truth, had slept little more than we) over the breakfast table."

Just as the story was completed, a rattle of wheels was heard in the driveway leading to the house. Presently a wagon drove up, containing — besides a short, thick-set man whom Randolph recognized as the sheriff, and the two young fellows who served as deputies — an Indian half covered in a blanket, a squaw, and two dignified brown pappooses. It was easy to recognize them as the Loon Pond campers.

CHAPTER III.

THE TRIAL.

IT was decided to give the Indians their dinner before examining them. Mr. Percival knew they would be more likely to tell the truth if well-treated; and all he wanted was to obtain the watch, not to punish the thieves. Accordingly they were conducted to the kitchen, and there, under charge of the sheriffs, they were provided with a bountiful meal by aunt Puss.

The captors meanwhile explained that they had found their prisoners encamped about ten miles down the road. They had been very angry at first, but the sheriff, who was really a good-natured farmer living about three miles from Mr. Percival's place, had managed to pacify Sebattis, the father of the family, and he kept Moll in good order. They all, added Mr. Blake, the sheriff, had denied any knowledge of the watch, from first to last.

After dinner, to which the Indians did ample

justice, the whole party were conducted to the sitting-room. Mr. Percival took his seat beside a table, at one end of the room, and asked Sebattis to hold up his right hand. He then administered the oath to the prisoner with a dignity and solemnity which impressed the young people, and which were specially admired by Randolph, who had several times seen the ceremony flippantly performed in the city courts.

The magistrate now proceeded with the examination.

"What is your name, sir?" he asked gravely but pleasantly.

The Indian, gratified by the title given him, answered with promptness: "Sebattis Megone."

"That is your wife with you?"

"Yis. She Moll Megone."

"Where have you been camping for the last month?"

Sebattis hesitated a moment, then glanced at his wife and replied, "Tent down by Loon Pond. No good. Bad place. Me leave him."

"What was the matter with the place?"

"No fish. Water bad drink."

"Then why didn't you go away before?"

Again the Indian paused, scowled slightly, and threw his blanket across his shoulder with a gesture not without dignity.

"Me go when like; stay when like."

Here Moll gave a sharp look at her husband, which Randolph was just in time to catch. Seeing that her glance was noticed, she made the best of it and spoke up boldly.

"We go sell baskit," she said. "Plenty folk in big town to buy 'em —"

"Wait a moment," interrupted Mr. Percival. "You shall tell your story in a moment. Eunice, you give this woman a comfortable place in the kitchen with her babies, will you?"

Both Indians seemed inclined to resent this move, but the magistrate was evidently not a man to be trifled with, and Moll sullenly withdrew, bearing a pappoose on each arm.

"Now," continued Mr. Percival once more, "did you, Sebattis, see any of these young people yesterday?"

"No. Me hunt on furder side Loon Pond."

"Did your wife tell you about it when you came back to the tent at night?"

"When me come wigwam, Moll say girl-with-gold-hair fall in pond, come near drown. Ver' hard make alive ag'in. That all."

"Didn't she show you something she had found?"

"Yis." And the Indian gravely held up his hand, making a circle with his thumb and forefinger.

"What was it?"

The children leaned forward expectantly, Pet's eyes sparkling.

The Indian never showed by the movement of a muscle nor a glance of the eye the irony with which he had purposely led his questioners to this point.

"Half dollar," he replied, in his slow, guttural tones. "Moll find it where white hunter, *that man*," indicating Ruel, who was standing near, "drop it in bushes when he go pray."

All turned and looked at Ruel, who flushed to his hair, but stood his ground.

"How do you know he prayed?" asked Mr. Percival gently.

"Wife find where he two knees go down on moss. Half dollar drop out. Wife say no keep. I say yis, keep him for work an' wet blankit."

Mr. Percival smiled in spite of himself at the man's confession; nevertheless he looked troubled.

"Do you mean to tell me, Sebattis," he said sternly, after a moment, "that you have never seen this girl's watch? If half a dollar fell out of a pocket, so could a watch. Come, my man, own up and give it back, and I'll let you go this time."

The Indian's brow darkened, and he drew himself up to his full height.

"Sebattis no see watch. Know nothing 'bout him."

He delivered himself of this remark with more emphasis than he had yet used; then sat down, pulling his blanket around him; and not another word would he speak, save a few guttural sentences in his own language to his wife, who was now called in once more. The scowl remained on his forehead, and Kittie whispered to Bess that she saw him eying the windows and their fastenings.

Moll was now sharply questioned, but with no better result. She had seen the gold watch-chain, she admitted, when the girls first reached the tent. It was dangling from *her* pocket — pointing to Kittie!

"O," cried Kittie, "but that's impossible, for I

haven't any watch nor chain myself, and I never even touched Pet's but once, and that was the day we all got here and she was showing it to aunt."

Mr. Percival looked grave; the sheriff shut one eye knowingly; the girls edged off, half-scared, after Kittie had spoken. Moll alone appeared to retain her perfect self-possession.

"It was in that one's pocket," she persisted, using much better English than her husband. "I was 'fraid pappooses grab it, and break. Maybe she take it," she added, with a malicious look at poor Kittie.

"Silence!" said uncle Will sternly. "Answer my questions, and nothing more. When did you say you saw this chain?"

"When gal first come."

"Not after they returned from the pond?"

"No. Forget all about it. Too much drown," said the squaw grimly. "Didn't see him no more." And no other answer nor admission could be obtained.

Ruel, Randolph and the girls were now asked a few questions each, to bring out their story in the hearing of the Indians. The latter denied nothing, and admitted nothing.

Mr. Percival looked perplexed. To him the guilt of the Indians seemed plain, especially after the palpable falsehood of the squaw. Nothing could have been easier, in the excitement of the restoration of the half-drowned girl, than to draw the watch from her cast-off clothes, and conceal it. The ground over which the party had passed had been scrutinized inch by inch, as well as the smooth, hard bottom of the lake where the accident had occurred; and by eyes that were as sharp as those of the Indians themselves. When Ruel said quietly after his morning search, that the watch was not in the woods nor the lake, that possibility was dropped, as settled beyond doubt. There had not been much ground to examine, for Pet distinctly remembered, and in this she was corroborated by Randolph, that she had taken out her watch and named the time of day, just before they first reached the wigwam.

Still, the magistrate could not commit the prisoners without some shadow of real proof; and he was obliged to admit to himself that there was none whatever. He called Mr. Blake aside, and held a consultation with him in low tones. The attention of the others was for the moment taken up with the pappooses, who were indulging themselves in various grunts and gasps and queer noises, accompanied by energetic struggles as if they were attacked by some internal foe, such as occasionally invades babyland. Moll sat holding them, sullen and silent.

"It must be a pin —" began aunt Puss, with a sympathetic movement toward the baby whose uncouth wails were the wildest; but she did not finish her sentence. A crashing of glass close at hand startled everybody in the room; and one glance at the shattered window-sash told the whole story. Sebattis, watching his opportunity, and seeing both doors of the room blocked by his persecutors, had sprung through the lower half of the window, carrying glass and all before him, and in an instant was out of sight in the forest.

The babies, strange to say, had become perfectly quiet and no one having seen the quick gleam of triumph in the squaw's eyes, she was not suspected of having been the cause of their previous outcries, by various sly pinches under the blanket.

The officers of the law at once sprang toward the door, but Mr. Percival checked them. "It's of no use," he said. "The only real misdemeanor that can be proved against the fellow is assault and battery on my window," he added, gazing ruefully at the ragged edges of the glass. "It rather relieves us, Blake, of the necessity of a decision in the watch matter, for you might scour the woods for a month without finding an Indian who wanted to keep out of the way."

"I only hope," said the sheriff, "that he won't lay it up against us, round here. These chaps are ugly enough to burn a barn, if no worse, for sheer revenge."

Here Ruel whispered to Mr. Percival, who proceeded to act at once upon what was evidently the guide's suggestion.

"Moll," he said to the squaw, who had watched the faces of the men with hardly concealed eagerness, "I'm sorry your husband ran away, for I should have let him go, anyway. Now these men will carry you back to your tent. If you ever find that watch," he added meaningly, looking her full in the eye, "bring it to me and you shall have twenty dollars reward."

Without a word the woman rose, and passing out, seated herself once more in the wagon, which drove off rapidly down the road in the direction of her wigwam. The trial was over, and the prisoners discharged; but the vexed question still remained, Where was the watch?

In the afternoon, while Ruel and Tim repaired the broken window — for panes of glass, putty and carpenter's tools were always ready at hand in the workshop — the boys walked over to the pond and examined the path and its vicinity carefully for themselves, and even took turns diving to the bottom of the pond, in a vain search for the missing article. Wherever it might be, it clearly had been carried off by some human agency. Pet's father and mother were at this time stopping in a large hotel near Boston, and had written for her to come up for a day or two, as there were friends visiting them from the West whom they were particularly anxious for her to meet and help entertain. She could return to Mr. Percival's, her mother wrote, by the middle of the following week.

With a sad heart, both at leaving her friends, and because she felt she was abandoning all hope of her watch, she started off early on the morning after the trial, with Ruel as driver, for the Pineville Station where she was to take the cars on a Branch of the Maine Central Railroad, for Boston.

All the young folks except Tom, who unexpectedly declined to go, on the plea of a headache, accompanied Pet to the station, telling her about their "Camp Christmas" of the preceding winter, and waving hats and handkerchiefs until the train rounded a curve and crept out of sight.

Meanwhile Tom languidly rose from his bed, as soon as he heard the laughing wagon-load drive away; went down to breakfast with a sulky face and red eyes, as if he had been up late the night before, or had been crying — and hardly waiting to reply to his uncle's cheery good-morning, walked off with his hands in his pockets, in the direction of Loon Pond. After an absence of a couple of hours, he returned, looking tired out, and passed the rest of the forenoon in the barn, lying on the hay-mow with a book. But if you had peeped over his shoulder, you would have seen that the pages were upside-down, and that now and then a tear rolled slowly over the boy's cheeks, while his lips twitched nervously. Tom was evidently, on this bright June day, one of the unhappiest of boys. What could have happened?

CHAPTER IV.

FIRE!

"I WONDER if they *are* so different!"
Pet Sibley found the summer hotel very pleasant. She was fond of gayety and pretty dresses and music; and of these she found a plenty at the "Everglades." The hotel was within a half-hour's ride of Boston, but was situated in the very heart of a beautiful, shadowy grove of pines, whose breath made the air sweet all through the long hours of the languid summer day. If the trees were more civilized and conventional in their appearance than the wide-branching, free-tossing pines in Uncle Percival's upland pastures and hundred-acre wood-lot, Pet was not yet enough waked-up to know the difference; in fact, found it rather nice to be able to stroll about the well-kept grounds of the "Everglades," without fear of tearing her skirts in the underbrush, or losing her way if she left the path. There was no under-

brush here, and it was pretty much all path.

Within a few minutes' walk, and bordering the grove on the further side, a river wound pleasantly and peacefully through a bright strip of meadowland. On this river the Sibleys kept a boat, with carpet and cushioned seats — not much like the rough little affair which had tipped Pet over into Loon Pond.

Life at the Everglades flowed softly and calmly, like the river; and on the surface floated, like its radiant lilies, the fair ladies, young and old, who fanned and smiled and danced away the summer, without a thought of the suffering thousands in the hot city, fifteen miles away.

Without a thought? Yes, there were some who thought, and who brought poor and ailing children out to a Country Home near by; but these were few.

Pet Sibley, I am glad to say, was one of those who remembered the narrow streets of the North End, and the swarms of ragged men, women and children who panted, dog-like, on curbstone and doorstep, along the foul streets as the sun went down each night.

The people from the West, Pet learned, were

relatives, and though their views of life hardly agreed with her own — if, indeed, she had any views — she found the new-comers very pleasant. On the third day after her return, her cousin Mark, whose home was in Chicago, and with whom already, in the free intimacy of hotel life, she felt well acquainted, had taken her out on the river.

A half-hour had slipped by, during which her cousin had instructed her how to sit safely in a boat, and even how to row a little. Just as they turned a bend in the stream and floated into a cove where birches and wild grape-vines afforded a grateful bit of shade, the girl stopped rowing, and looking up at Mark, who sat indolently in the stern of the boat, made the remark with which this chapter began:

"I wonder if they are so — *different!*"

Pet's pretty young forehead had a puzzled little wrinkle as she leaned forward, with the oar-blades rippling through the water, and the muslin sleeves falling back from her brown wrists.

"*Are* they so different, cousin Mark?"

Her companion gave an impatient twitch to his straw hat.

"Why, of course! They are not like you, Pet.

They are ignorant and poor and — and not clean, you know. They were born to it and they like it."

"But it doesn't seem right. I heard a lady on the piazza this morning say something about 'those creatures' in such a way that I thought she was speaking of rats or snakes. It turned out she meant the convicts who attacked their keepers at the prison last July."

Pet spoke warmly, as she was apt to do when she once took up a subject. If she was yet a gay young creature, very fond of "good times," and ready for any sort of fun, she yet was one of those girls with whom shallow young men at summer hotels are rather shy of entering into conversation. She was only fifteen, and one by one the terribly real problems of the day were marshalling themselves before her. She would not pass them by with a gay laugh, after the prevailing mode of her merry companions. She felt somehow that it belonged to her to help the world and make it better, as well as to the missionaries and other good people upon whose shoulders we so willingly pack responsibilities.

For this childish enthusiasm she was smiled on indulgently by her friends. Kitty and Bess knew the best there was in her, and loved her for it.

Pet gave two or three quick strokes, and paused.

"Isn' there any way to help these poor people, Mark? It must be the way these people live and are brought up that makes them so rough and bad. Isn't there any way to help them?"

"None that amounts to much. Besides, that isn't our business. There are men enough who do nothing else — are paid for it — missionaries and the like. And you can't make everybody rich, you know. The Bible itself says, 'Ye have the poor always with you.'"

"Perhaps that doesn't mean that we ought to have them," replied Pet, slowly.

"Well, they're here, and we may as well make the best of it."

"But what is the best? That's just it."

"What is the use of your thinking about it? You can't do anything, and you don't even know the kind of people we're talking of; the North-Enders, for instance. You have never seen and touched them; and if you should meet them face to face, I don't believe you would care for any further acquaintance. They're simply disgusting."

Pet said no more on the subject, and just as the sun dropped into the arms of the waiting pines on the hill they reached the little wharf on the riverbank, moored the boat, and walked up to the hotel. She went straight to her mother's room, and, after her fashion, as straight to the point.

"Mother, I want to go into the city right away, and spend the night with aunt Augusta."

"But, my child, it's tea-time already, and there's a hop this evening. You had better wait till morning."

"Mother, I so much want to go now. The train leaves in fifteen minutes. I don't care for the hop, anyway; it's too warm to dance. Please, mother?"

Of course impulsive little Pet had her way, and was soon whirling along toward the city, with a strong resolve in her mind.

"I'll walk up to auntie's from the depot, and tomorrow I'll go down to North Street with uncle."

The train stopped at all the small stations, and was delayed by various causes, so that it was quite dark when she started on her walk. She was glad, after all, to find the streets well-lighted, and filled with respectable-looking people.

On reaching Washington Street, however, everything appeared weird and unnatural. The sidewalks along which one could hardly pass in the daytime, for the crowd, were nearly deserted. All the spots that were bright by sunlight, were now dark, and all the ordinarily dark places light. It was exactly like the negative of a photograph, and gave Pet a sense of looking on the wrong side of everything. Once she saw something move behind the broad plate-glass windows of a railroad agency, on a corner that in the daytime was a business centre. She approached, and was startled to find the object a huge rat, trotting silently about, over the polished engravings and placards, behind the glass, a very spirit of solitude and evil. It was all like a nightmare, and she began most heartily to wish herself back at the Everglades, dancing the Lancers with cousin Mark.

Coincidences happen; not in stories simply, but in real life. The vessel is wrecked in sight of port; the day the owner dies; the man we meet on the steamboat at the headwaters of the Saguenay River, has, unknown to us until then, ate, drank, and slept in the next house all winter, within ten feet of us; the dear friend we have known so long, is at last discovered to be intimate with that other dear friend we love so well, and finally it comes out that all three of us were born in the same little town in New Hampshire.

Now the coincidence that happened on this particular evening was as follows:

While Pet was making her way along Washington Street in the dark, another girl about thirteen years of age, named Bridget Flanagan, was standing on the third gallery of the Crystal Palace, in the same good city of Boston, looking down into Lincoln Street. Like Pet, she was wondering whether anything could be done to aid the poor. Not that any such words passed through her mind. Dear me, no! I doubt if she would have even known what "aid" meant, that word being in her mind associated solely with lemons of a shrivelled and speckled character. If she had spoken her thoughts, which she sometimes had a queer way of doing, she might have said something like this: "Don't I wish I could git out o' this! An' the rich folks wid all the money they wants, an' nothin' to do but buy fans an' use 'em up. My! ain't it hot?"

It *was* hot. There was a man playing on a bagpipe in the street below, and not only had a crowd of children and idlers surrounded him as he stood before a brilliantly lighted (and licensed) liquor store, but the long rickety galleries which run in front of each floor in the "Palace" were full of half-dressed, red-faced women and children, who leaned on the dirty railing and listened to the music, just as the guests at the "Everglades" at the same time were listening to their orchestra of a dozen pieces.

In the gallery overhead Bridget heard two women dancing and shouting noisily. Somewhere in the building a child was crying loudly in a different key from the bag-pipe. Bridget didn't notice these things particularly; she was used to them. Only there came over the young human girl-heart which was beating beneath the rags and in the midst of this wretchedness a sick longing for — what? Bridget did not know.

"It's the hot weather it is," she said to herself; "it's usin' me up intirely. I'll jist go an' have a bit av a walk."

Accordingly she issued forth, shortly afterward, with a broken-nosed pitcher in her hand, and made her way to one of the shops across the street. There were plenty to choose from — the city had looked out for that. Their licenses were as strong as the Municipal Seal, stamped on one corner, with its picture of church steeples and clouds, and heavens above and pure, broad sea beneath, could make them. Nearly every second house in the street beckoned with flaring lights to its pile of whiskey barrels and shining counters; the dark intervals along the street, between these shops, were the ruined homes of those who went in at the lighted doors.

Opposite, the Crystal Palace, then at its filthiest and worst, reared its ugly shape like a fat weed, watered day and night by whiskey and gin.

[Within the last twelvemonth this building has been torn down, and Lincoln Street largely reclaimed from the squalor and wretchedness which marked it on the evening of which I am speaking; but within a stone's throw of the same spot, the same sights may be witnessed any night in the week. The district is popularly known as the "South Cove."]

As Bridget pattered along the sidewalk with her bare feet, a coarse-looking woman in front of her threw something down on the bricks and laughed hoarsely. The "something" resolved itself into a kitten, which picked itself up and walked painfully over to a burly, broad-shouldered man who was sitting on the steps of a basement alley, so that his arms rested on the sidewalk. The kitten curled up beside him. The man put out his big, red hand and stroked it once, then went on with his smoking. The kitten was purring and licking its aching feet as Bridget, who had paused a moment from some dull feeling of compassion, went on her way.

Leaving her pitcher at the bar, with the injunction that it should be filled and ready for her return, she passed out of the store and walked slowly down Lincoln Street toward the Albany Station. The street was full of children running to and fro with shouts and screams of laughter or pain; some of them going in and out of the shops with pitchers and mugs, some lying stupidly in the gutter. The air was stifling, and as Bridget reached the corner she saw the groups of belated people hurrying out to the Newtons and Wellesley, where they might cool themselves in the pure air, with whatever means of comfort money could purchase.

Pet Sibley and Bridget Flanagan both reflected upon this as they unconsciously drew nearer and nearer together. Pet was tired, and was beginning to look for a horse-car to take her to her aunt's house. The little Irish princess had turned and left her "Palace" until she was now near the head of Summer Street.

Ten steps further, and they met upon the corner, with the great gilded eagle's wings outstretched above their heads. Both paused for a moment. Pet was dressed as she had been in the boat — all in white, with a pretty fluffy ostrich feather curving around her broad straw hat, and a fleecy shawl thrown over her shoulders. Bridget's shawl was not fleecy, and her dress was not white. Nor did she wear lawn shoes.

What either would have said I do not know. Perhaps nothing. Perhaps their lives, just touching at this point, would have glided farther and farther apart, until there was no room in this earth for them to meet again. But at that moment something happened.

"Look o' that!" cried Bridget.

"See!" cried Pet at the same moment; and they both pointed to the third story of a high granite block across the street. One of the windows was slightly open, and through this narrow space a delicate curl of blue smoke floated softly out, laughed noiselessly to itself, and disappeared. They could hardly have seen it at all, but for the powerful electric light upon the corner. Another puff of smoke, and another; then a steady stream, growing blacker and larger every moment. A faint glow, reflected from somewhere inside, shone upon the window panes.

"What shall we do?" cried Pet; "it's all on fire, and nobody knows!" Instinctively she looked at Bridget for an answer. Somehow the difference between herself and the ragged little Irish girl did not seem so great just then.

The fire had broken out near the place where the great fire of 1872 started. Each of the girls could remember dimly that awful night of red skies and glittering steeples. The massive blocks had been rebuilt, business had rolled through the streets once more, property of value untold lay piled away in those great warehouses on every side, and only these two slender, wide-eyed girls knew of that ugly black smoke, with its gleaming tongues of flame, gliding about over counter and shelf, as Pet had seen the rat, a few minutes before.

"Sure we must give the alar-r-m," said Bridget,

hurriedly, gathering the faded shawl about her neck.

"But I don't know how. Do you?"

"Don't I? You jist come along wid me — run, now!"

They almost flew down the street, dainty shoes and bare brown feet side by side.

"Here's the box," panted Bridget, pausing suddenly before an iron box attached to a telegraph pole. "Can yer read where it says the key is?"

Pet read: "Key at Faxon's Building, corner of Bedford and Summer Streets."

To reach the corner, rouse the watchman, snatch the key from his sleepy hands, rush back again, and whisk open the iron box was the work of two minutes.

Perfect silence everywhere.

"Look a-here, now," said Bridget, breathlessly, standing on tiptoe. "I've seen 'em do it."

She pulled the handle once, twice. Then they waited, their hearts beating fiercely. They were off the travelled ways, and no one passed by them. All this time the smoke was creeping up the stairways of the lofty building, and the red fire was quietly devouring yard after yard of wood-work.

Bridget raised her hand to pull the lever for the third and last time — when they both started.

All over the broad, restless, wakeful city, the heavy bells rang out, one following another like echoes. Sick people turned wearily in their beds; babies awoke to bewail their broken naps; men and women stopped at the corners of streets to count the number, and shook their heads.

"Bad place, down by Summer and Chauncey Streets — let's go!" said one to another.

One — Two — Three — Four — Five — One — Two.

Miss Augusta Vernon consulted her fire-alarm card, which always hung by the sitting-room mantel-piece; then she went to the front window and threw open the blinds. There was a faint flush on the sky, like the coming dawn.

"Dear me!" exclaimed aunt Augusta. "It's a real fire. And this hot night, too! I do hope they'll have it out soon, poor fellows!"

As she took her seat by the window, and watched the light growing broader and redder every moment, her strong, kind features showed much more anxiety than one would expect, considering that it was not her store that was burning, nor her firemen fighting the fire. But aunt Augusta, in the city, had a curious way like that of aunt Puss up in the Maine woods, of concerning herself with other people's troubles and trying to lighten them, with loving-kindness or with money. As she had a plentiful supply of both, her sympathy in such cases was apt to be a substantial affair, really worth counting upon — as many a poor creature, sick and in prison, could testify.

As soon as the bells rang out, a great awe fell upon the two girls. What mighty host of giants had they roused from sleep, calling hoarsely to one another over the housetops?

Pet drew closer to Bridget, and grasped her hand. Even Bridget seemed dismayed at first, but quickly recovering herself, she half pushed, half drew Pet up a flight of high stone steps near by.

"Yer'll git yer dress all kivered wid mud, if yer don't kape out o' the strate," she said, as she turned away. "I'm a-goin' ter stay down an' tell 'em where the fire is. It says so on them little cards."

"But the crowd! When they come you will get hurt."

"Hm! I'm used to worse crowds nor ever you saw. There! I hear 'em now!"

As Pet listened there rose a faint, far-off rattle of wheels upon the pavement, mingled with a jangling sound of gongs and horns.

"It's the ingine!" cried Bridget, in great excitement. "It's comin'!"

But other things were coming too. Bridget had taken her stand directly in front of the alarm-box, and a stream of men and boys who poured around the corner jostled her roughly and pushed her to and fro.

"Come!—come quick!" called Pet, just able to make herself heard above the noise of the crowd. But Bridget shook her head, and pointed down the street.

It was a grand sight— the engine, with its scarlet wheels, and its polished stack sending out a long trail of brilliant sparks like shooting stars, the two powerful black horses tearing furiously over the pavements, yet subject to the slightest word or touch of their driver, who sat behind them firmly braced against the foot-board, the reins taut as steel, and the gong sounding beneath without pause.

"Get out of the way here!" shouted a burly policeman, forcing his way through the crowd.

FIRE! 69

The men surged back, and nobody noticed the little barefooted figure who was hurled violently against the building. She uttered a faint cry, and held up one foot, as a lame spaniel might do. A young man with delicate clothes and a light cane, who had stopped on his way to the station to "see the fun," had set his heavy boot on the little, shrinking foot. She might have got out of the way more quickly, but she *must* keep to the front to tell the firemen.

The engine thundered up to the box and stopped, hissing and smoking furiously. The black horses quivered and pawed the pavement, shaking white flecks of foam over their sleek bodies.

"Where's the fire?" called the driver sharply.

"Blest if I know—" began one of the men addressed, but he was interrupted.

"Sure it's on Summer Street, sir, 'most up to Washington, on the other side."

It was a surprisingly small, shrill voice for such an important piece of information, but it sounded reliable. The driver knew that every moment now might mean the loss of thousands of dollars, and, giving his horses the rein, was galloping off up the street again, almost before Bridget's words were out of her mouth. A few moments after, the panting engine and the distant shouts of the firemen told of the work they were doing.

Well, the block was saved. A few thousand dollars' damage on goods fully insured was all. Next morning the papers, being somewhat hard pressed for news, gave "full particulars" of the fire.

"It was fortunate," said the eloquent reporter, in closing his account, "that the fire was discovered by some passer-by, who promptly pulled in an alarm from box fifty-two. Five minutes later, and the loss must have been almost incalculable."

"Full particulars?" Perhaps not quite full.

When the engine rattled away, with the crowd after it, Pet had come timidly down the steps. Bridget had been borne away by the crowd, and was not to be found.

"Where are you?" she called. "I do not know your name — oh-h!" She stopped with a pitiful little cry.

Bridget was crouched in a miserable heap just around the corner. She was stroking her bruised foot with trembling hands, and crying softly to herself. Somehow she felt like the kitten, only she had no one to go to; and her head was so dizzy!

Then she looked up, and saw the white shawl and the ostrich feather and Pet's eyes. And once more Pet forgot the difference.

A policeman found them there a few minutes later. Pet had her arms around the faded shawl, and Bridget's tously little head was lying wearily against her shoulder. The poor trampled foot was bound up in somebody's embroidered handkerchief.

Pet did not give the officer time to speak. She was on her own ground now.

"Will you call a hack or a herdic, please? This girl is sick."

The tone was quiet, but plainly said it was accustomed to giving directions, and having them obeyed, too.

The policeman had approached with a rough joke on his tongue's end, but it turned into a respectful "Yes'm, certainly."

Of course they went straight to aunt Augusta, who was still sitting by the window, and who was so used to emergencies that she took the whole affair quite as a matter of course.

"I've told the Lord I'm not worth it," she had been heard to say, once, "but such as I am, I want to help. So I'm always expecting Him to give me something of the sort, just as my father used to let me hold the tacks when he was at work on pictures or carpets."

Bridget was promptly put to bed and her foot dressed by Miss Augusta's own deft hands. Before long she was fast asleep, which probably didn't make much difference with her state of mind, as the whole scene, with Pet and the motherly woman hovering about her, was the best kind of a dream.

Meanwhile Pet told the story to her aunt; she had learned from the Irish girl, on the way to the house, that she had no father or mother living, but made her home with a dissipated uncle and brother, who took turns in the prisoner's dock of the criminal court; where, likely enough, Bridget would have taken her own turn, before long.

"I know what I'm going to do," said Miss Augusta, decisively. "I'm going to send her up to Mrs. Percival. When are you going back, Pet?"

"Day after to-morrow, I think."

"Well, you can take her along as well as not."

"But her family —"

"I'll see Mr. Waldron — he's the City Missionary — and he'll fix it all right. We've often arranged matters like this."

"But do you suppose Mrs. Percival will take her?" asked Pet rather doubtfully.

"I don't see 's she can help it," said Miss Augusta, with a short laugh. "Don't you fear. I know 'aunt Puss' better than you do, though I never 've seen her. Kittie and Bess told me all about her, last spring." So it came about that when Pet took her seat in the Northern train, a few days later, a neatly dressed little Irish girl sat beside her, awed into silence by the furniture of the car and, shortly afterward, by its rapid motion.

When the conductor came round for the tickets, her hand furtively stole over and clutched a fold of Pet's rich dress, for protection from the man in uniform. And Pet had to reassure her, and point out interesting bits of landscape as they flew northward toward The Pines, side by side.

CHAPTER V.

IN THE DEN.

AT The Pines, during Pet's absence, the summer days passed swiftly and joyously; joyously at least for all but one of the party. Tom was no longer the bright, merry, mischievous Tom of old. He joined in the sports and rambles of the others, it is true, but with a sober face and lagging step quite unnatural for him; and he was often away from the house, alone. As these strange ways grew more marked, Randolph tried to get at at the source of the boy's trouble. But Tom shrugged his cousin's arm off from his shoulders where it had been affectionately laid, and told him gruffly to "let a fellow alone — nothing was the matter!"

It was almost time for Pet to return. The young people had arranged to ride over to the railroad and meet her, with Ruel and the big wagon. They had received a letter from her, telling a little about her experience at the fire, and they were extremely anxious to hear the whole story, and to see little Bridget, the heroine of the occasion. Mr. Waldron, with his great, kindly heart, had given Miss Augusta all the aid she asked, and more; so there was no obstacle in the way of Bridget's coming, unless it were aunt Puss. And the idea of aunt Puss being an obstacle — !

On the day before, Kittie and the captain had planned to go into the woods and gather oak leaves for trimming, to decorate Pet's room. What was their dismay, on waking that morning, to hear the rain pouring steadily on the shingles over their heads.

"Now we can't get any leaves!" exclaimed Bess sorrowfully, as she stood at the window, looking out at the blurred landscape and the slanting lines of rain between her and the wood-lot. "What ever *shall* we do, all day?"

"O, I don't know," laughed Kittie, giving her sister's long brown hair a toss up backward and down over her eyes. "Uncle Percival will think of something nice, I guess. And I'm glad the storm didn't come to-morrow, anyway!"

"Perhaps it will."

"Perhaps it won't!" Kittie's face and voice were full of sunshine.

"That's right, Kittlin'," said aunt Puss, coming in at that moment, and kissing the girls. "That's right, dear, always look on the bright side; and if you can't find it in to-day, borrow it from to-morrow. The Bible doesn't anywhere say, 'sufficient unto the day is the *good* thereof.'"

"Please, ma'am," said Kittie, returning the kiss affectionately, "what did you call me?"

"It's the old Scotch form of 'kitten,'" said aunt Puss, smiling. "I first came across it in George MacDonald's story of Alec Forbes — which you both must read before you're much older."

The sunshine from Kittie's face began to rest on Bess, and to shine back a little.

"That's what Kit always does, auntie," she declared; "looks on the bright side. When anybody's sick at our house, and there's no particular change, she always says to people that inquire, 'No worse, thank you!' instead of 'No better,' the way some folks do."

At the kitchen table, the subject was started up again, and Randolph volunteered one of the little rhymes his brother had written. It was as follows:

THE WEST WINDOW.

DANDELION.

A dandelion in a meadow grew
    Among the waving grass and cowslips yellow;
Dining on sunshine, breakfasting on dew,
    He was a right contented little fellow.

Each morn his golden head he lifted straight
    To catch the first sweet breath of coming day;
Each evening closed his sleepy eyes, to wait
    Until the long, dark night should pass away.

One afternoon, in sad, unquiet mood,
    I passed beside this tiny, bright-faced flower,
And begged that he would tell me, if he could,
    The secret of his joy through sun and shower.

He looked at me with open eyes, and said:
    "I know the sun is somewhere shining clear,
And when I cannot see him overhead,
    I try to be a little sun, right here!"

When the applause had ceased, and the talk had drifted in other directions, Mr. Percival looked around the circle and with a twinkle in his eye proposed that after breakfast the young people should make him a visit in his den.

"And we'll have a rag fire," he added soberly.

" A *rag* fire?"

"Yes. In the summer time I rarely burn anything but rags in the den."

Now this "Den" was a most mysterious locality, which they had often heard alluded to, but where little company was admitted. Mr. Percival, I should add, was, as you may have guessed from aunt Puss' remarks about the "kittlin'," a most earnest reader and lover of George MacDonald's books, which perhaps accounts for the curious arrangement I am about to describe.

"Are we to put on our wraps, Uncle?" asked Kittie, in some doubt whether the Den was out-of-doors. "O, I *wish* Pet was here!"

"Pet shall come too, the very first rainy day. No; you'll need no wraps, dear. Only follow me softly, and don't speak aloud!" And his eyes twinkled again as he led the way out of the kitchen, and toward the front part of the house.

I have already, in the former volume of this series, partly described this old "mansion-house" which the Percivals had occupied for generations. The earliest of the family, Sir Richard Percyvalle, came over from the north of England in 1690 or thereabouts. Half a Scotchman, he brought with him alike the love of wild country, and of the ancient castles and baronial halls so dear to the Englishman. This "mansion-house," as it was called throughout the county, situated in the heart of a pine forest, near rugged hills and dancing brooks, was the result. And here some branch of the Percival stock had lived contentedly ever since, respected and loved by their few neighbors; some, indeed, finding their way to the great cities and universities and even back across the Atlantic, in pursuit of their education and professional studies; but at least one manly representative of the family always inhabiting the old house, which stood as stanchly as ever against the blasts of the North Wind and the rigors of the New England winter. It had all sorts of wings, ells and additions built on, extending the original structure as the occupant's whims or needs demanded. The portion in actual use by the family throughout the year was but a small fraction of the whole house.

The injunction not to speak aloud considerably increased the fun as well as the awe of the occasion, as Randolph, with his cousins, followed their uncle in a dumb but not altogether silent row.

Leaving the kitchen, they crossed a narrow passage-way leading into the sitting-room. Beyond this was a sort of closet or cloak-room, and then the front entry, a cold, cheerless place with a green fan-light over the door which was now entirely disused.

"Here the carriages used to drive up in ancient days," said Mr. Percival, "the postilions cracking their whips and the clumsy wheels lumbering heavily over the driveway. Then elegant ladies would alight, and passing through the open door ascend that staircase, their long gowns, stiff with silk and brocade, trailing behind them. Hark! Do you hear them rustling past us and up the stairs?"

The girls listened, partly for the fun of the thing, and partly because of the impressiveness of their uncle's manner. The rain beat drearily upon the door, and long, hanging vines brushed against it on the outside. Within, it was so dark that they could scarcely distinguish the staircase.

On they went again, up the very stairs the bygone beauties had ascended, through two broad chambers whose shutters were closed and nailed tight. Then down again, over a narrow flight of steps, and along a crooked passage, so dark that they had to feel their way.

Kittie laughed nervously, as she clutched Bessie's hand.

"Did you ever see anything like it!" she whispered. "I feel exactly as if I were in a story."

"I wish we'd stayed in the kitchen," said Tom. "What's the good of coming into this dark hole? I'm going back." And in spite of the remonstrances of the others, he turned and retraced his steps.

The sound of his footfalls, echoing down the the passage, made the place drearier than ever.

"Hush!" said Mr. Percival, out of the darkness. "Listen!"

They paused and strained their ears to catch a sound above that of the storm, whose dull roar beat indistinctly, like ocean waves, on the gables overhead.

"I hear something!" exclaimed Randolph under his breath, entering fully into the spirit of the adventure.

"So do I!" said both girls at once. "It's a kind of creaking, snapping noise!"

"Here," added Mr. Percival solemnly, throwing open a door they had not before perceived, "is the entrance to the Den."

The room into which they now emerged from

the narrow entry was apparently once intended for a dining-hall, though the young people had never before known of even its existence. It was of oblong shape, and had at one end a huge fireplace. The windows were heavily shuttered; the air was damp and musty. In the dim light they could make out clusters of old-fashioned candelabra, projecting here and there from the walls like spectral arms.

"Come on!" said Mr. Percival, advancing toward the end of the shadowy room. To the surprise of all three, he walked straight into the fireplace, stooping but slightly to avoid the mantel. The rest followed him, wondering. The snapping noise was now louder than ever. Outside, the wind moaned drearily.

Mr. Percival now turned sharply to the left and pressed with the flat of his hand against a projecting brick upon that side of the fireplace.

What was the utter amazement of Randolph and the girls, as they crowded up to discover what he was about, to see — not a brick wall where had been one a moment before, but mere black space.

"Come on!" said their uncle again, stepping into the opening.

Randolph went in after him, and the girls next, not without their misgivings.

"It's exactly like a dream!"

"Or the Arabian Nights. Pinch me, Bess, to see if I'm asleep!"

As soon as they found themselves in the new passage, they heard the wall close behind them. Half a dozen steps further, and —

"This is my Den!" said Mr. Percival.

The girls rubbed their eyes, and stared silently. This is what they saw:

A small room, perhaps ten feet square. One window, with a deep casement, making a window-seat at least two feet wide. A warm-tinted carpet on the floor, where three Maltese kittens tumbled over each other in solemn play; walls lined with books from floor to ceiling; an open fire of twigs and stiff birch bark, blazing cheerily in a wee fireplace — and in front of it, rocking serenely to and fro with her knitting, aunt Puss! She looked up with her pleasant smile as the young people entered.

"He gave you a good surprise this time, dears, didn't he?"

"I never saw anything like it!" they exclaimed

in a breath. "How in the world did *you* get here, ma'am?"

Mrs. Percival looked at her husband, who took his seat in the large, old-fashioned arm-chair which played an important part during the "Pine Cone stories" in the winter; at the same time motioning to the others to lie down on a bear-skin rug, before the fire. It must be borne in mind that in Northern Maine it is cool enough for fires, on stormy days, throughout the year.

"I suppose," he began, "it's of no use making a mystery of it any longer. The fact is, you are in a chimney at this minute. Look!"

He pointed to the ceiling, which they now noticed was of some dark wood. In the centre, or nearly so, was an opening, about eighteen inches square and cased in the same wood, through which they could see the sky. The opening was covered at the top, far above the level of the ceiling, by a dull, glazed window, which could be raised or closed from below by means of strong cords.

"But what — what has become of the fire and the bricks, and all that, sir?"

"I'll tell you," said uncle Will, stooping to pick up two of the kittens in one hand. "In old times,

"SHE HAD ONE PAPPOOSE IN HER ARMS."

when my great-grandfather lived here, there was always danger of attack of some kind. The woods were full of Indians, though most of them hereabout were friendly, and there was a large Indian village on the shores of the pond, where the old gentleman and his family were held in equal love and respect. However, roving bands were likely to turn up at any time, with tomahawk and scalping-knife. Then there were privateering squads of outlaw French and Canadians, who made raids on the frontier; and as we were always stanch Whigs, the family was not safe even from the English, the royalist partisans having suspicions of a spy in this locality."

"I thought 'Whigs' were the government party in England," put in Randolph.

"So they are, to-day; but in the old Revolutionary times the Tories were for the king, and the Whigs for independence. Well, for all these reasons, it was thought best to have some secret hiding-place and way of escape, in case of need. Where we are now, stood a huge chimney, some eight feet square, supported on stone-and-brick arches in the cellar. Around this chimney, as a precaution against fire, was left a space of two or three feet between the bricks and the wall of the house on that side where you see my little window. A sliding door was constructed in the side of the dining-hall fireplace, by which one could enter this space, and from that a trap-door opened upon a rough staircase, into the cellar under the masonry."

"It doesn't seem possible that such things can really be, right here in Maine!" exclaimed Bess. "It's like stories."

"If they can really be — as they are — in thousands of ancient dwellings in Europe and the East, why not in America, where the dangers were quite as terrible? Besides, dear, you will find out some day that the real life of people going on everywhere around you is much more strange than any story-book you ever read."

"But please, wouldn't one starve or smother in that place down cellar?"

"From the narrow space under the arches, I am told there led a long, underground passage-way, which came to the surface within a quarter of a mile of the house. I always fancied it was in the pasture, but never could find it. This end was tightly closed up — if indeed the whole passage-way was not an empty tale — years before I was born."

"And what has become of the chimney?"

"It was taken out as useless and unsafe, when I was a boy. A few years ago it occurred to me to wall in and fit up the space as a little study. The ordinary entrance is from the sitting-room closet, only ten feet from where you sit now. That is the way your aunt Puss came in."

The girls gave a relieved laugh as the vague terrors of the winding and shadowy halls melted.

"It's as cosey as it can be," said Kittie, stroking one of her namesakes, and glancing over the books, the writing desk in one corner, and the dancing flames.

"But the rags, the rags!" cried Bess. "You said you only burned rags, Uncle. Now I've caught you!"

"Randolph," remarked Mr. Percival, without directly answering her question, "will you please hand me that small book on the third shelf behind you — no, the next — that's it."

He ran the leaves over rapidly, and handed the book back, open, to the boy. "Please read that verse. The writer, who you will see is Mr. Trowbridge, is supposed to be searching the woods for a bird whose song he has just heard."

Randolph turned his back a little to the fire, as he lay on the bear-skin, and read as follows:

> Long-drawn and clear its closes were —
>   As if the hand of Music through
>   The sombre robe of silence drew
> A thread of golden gossamer;
>   So pure a flute the fairy blew.
> Like beggared princes of the wood,
> In silver rags the birches stood;
> The hemlocks, lordly counselors,
> Were dumb; the sturdy servitors,
> In beechen jackets patched and gray,
> Seemed waiting spell-bound all the day
> That low, entrancing note to hear, —
>   "*Pe-wee! pe-wee! peer!*"

The reader looked up, and seeing the interested faces of his listeners, begged leave to read two more verses, they were so quaintly lovely:

> I quit the search, and sat me down
>   Beside the brook, irresolute,
>   And watched a little bird in suit
> Of sombre olive, soft and brown,
>   Perched in the maple branches, mute;
> With greenish gold its vest was fringed,
> Its tiny cap was ebon tinged,
> With ivory pale its wings were barred,
> And its dark eyes were tender-starred.

> "Dear bird," I said, "what is thy name?"
> And twice the mournful answer came,
> So faint and far, and yet so near, —
> > "*Pewee! pewee! peer!*"
>
> For so I found my forest bird, —
>   The pewee of the loneliest woods,
>   Sole singer in these solitudes,
> Which never robin's whistle stirred,
>   Where never blue-bird's plume intrudes.
> Quick darting through the dewy morn,
> The redstart trilled his twittering horn
> And vanished in thick boughs; at even
> Like liquid pearls fresh showered from heaven,
> The high notes of the lone wood-thrush
> Fell on the forest's holy hush;
> But thou all day complainest here, —
> > "*Pewee! pewee! peer!*"

"It *is* lovely!" said Bess.

"There's one word in it that I don't like, though," remarked aunt Puss, making her needles gleam in the firelight as they flew faster than ever.

"I know," cried Kittie, catching her eye, "it's 'complainest'!"

Just then Tom came in, evidently from the guidance of Ruel, outside. His sisters were too much interested in the room and the poem to notice that his clothes were wet, as if he had been in the rain.

"Better come up by the fire, old fellow," said Randolph, so quietly that the others did not hear. Tom started, but did as his cousin suggested, without a word.

"You are right, dear," continued aunt Puss, "no bird ever 'complains'."

"Oh! but it's just poetry, you know, Aunt," said Bess eagerly. "Of course the birds don't *really* complain —"

"Good poetry is always true," said Mr. Percival. "Your aunt seems to me quite right, my girl. The lovely things that our Father has made should not be described as 'complaining,' even in fancy. After what is said in the Book, about sparrows, surely no bird ought to complain even of falling to the ground. The real secret of it was, I suspect, that the writer was himself in an unquiet mood, and made the 'little bird in suit of sombre olive' sing out his own discontent — as we are very apt to do."

"But the rags — O, I see, I see, it's just birch-bark hanging on the trunks and boughs of the trees!"

"Let me see," said uncle Percival, smiling, "whose favorite tree was the white birch, when we were talking around our pine-cone fire last winter?"

"Mine," said Bess. "But I never thought of the bark as 'silver rags'; nor of the trees as princes."

"Why not have a silver-rag story as well as pine-cone stories?" asked Randolph. "We can throw on bits of bark to keep the fire up, just as we did the cones; we only want a little blaze, anyway."

"I was afraid of it, I was afraid of it!" exclaimed Mr. Percival in mock-dismay. "I think I have an engagement in the lower pasture!"

An immediate assault followed, from which the good-natured old man rescued himself at last, breathless and rumpled, on promise of a story. Several broad sheets of birch-bark were drawn from a little cupboard beside the fireplace and given to the girls, who tore them into thin, silky strips, to be tossed on the fire during the progress of the story.

CHAPTER VI.

A SMALL HERO.

"DID you ever hear how a small boy — a very small boy indeed — saved Holland?" began Mr. Percival, after reflecting a moment.

"O no, sir. Is it a true story?"

"Absolutely true, with the exception, perhaps, of the name."

"We never heard of him, anyway."

"If you were a set of Dutch young people, you would have! The boy Hans, that did this brave deed, was a far finer fellow than Casabianca, who 'stood on the burning deck,' and supposed his father wanted him to burn to death for nothing but sheer obedience. For Hans accomplished something by his grand courage and endurance; he saved a whole nation!"

"Do tell us about him. Kittie, throw on another piece of bark, and don't let that cunning little Maltee tumble into the fire!"

"Well, Holland, you see, is a queer place. Hundreds of years ago people came upon a great swampy piece of land, running far out into the sea, and said, 'Now if we could only keep out the ocean in some way, this would be a nice place to live in. We could have towns and cities all along the coast, and we could build ships to sail around the world, and at last we should become so powerful that any nation would be glad to call us friends.'

"Accordingly they set their wits to work to devise some plan for holding back the salt tides, which rose and fell as they pleased all through the borders of this country. Then they began to build huge mounds of earth, or 'dykes,' along the shore; and they kept on building until they had a strong earthen wall nearly or quite around their land. Randolph, do you know any similar place in the Western Continent?"

"In some parts of Nova Scotia, I believe, sir."

"And along the Mississippi," added Tom.

"Right, both of you. The result was that the sea could no longer flood the fields, but threw its great waves and white foam against the outside of the dykes as if it were always trying to push its way in. As soon as people were sure their farms would not be washed away and their cattle drowned, they built towns, which grew and prospered amazingly. There was so little high land that there were but few streams powerful enough to turn 1-wheels, so they made wind-mills to grind their wheat and corn. Finally the country was named 'Holland,' and, as the first dyke-builders had expected, great nations were glad to win their good-will.

"Not many years ago there lived in Holland a small boy, rather strong for his age and size, whom we will call Hans Van Groot. His home was near the sea; and after he had attended to all his duties about home, he liked nothing better than to take a walk with his father along the top of the dyke, and watch the white cows, as he called the foamy waves, come rushing up to the shore, shaking their heads and bellowing at him.

"'No, no!' he would cry out, laughing gleefully, 'you can't get in, you can't get in! The fence is too strong for you!'

"He might well say so; for this was a peculiarly dangerous point on the coast, and the people knew that if the ocean should break the dyke all

Holland would be in peril, and thousands of lives, as well as no end of valuable property, would be lost. So they had made the sea-wall doubly thick and high for several miles in each direction."

"I've seen the waves dash up that way on Star Island, at the Shoals," said Bess. "They are awful, after a storm."

"On one of these quiet evening walks Hans' father had been talking to him about little faults.

"'If you do wrong once, my boy,' he said, 'no matter how little a wrong it is, there will some other bad thing be pretty apt to follow it; and so all the good in you may be swept away, bit by bit, until it is almost impossible to stop it.'

"'But it could be stopped very easily at first, father, you mean?'

"'Yes, Hans; just as you could stop with one finger a tiny leak in this dyke, which before morning would be a roaring flood so strong that no human power could hold it back. And Holland would be lost.'

"Hans pondered over this a great deal, in his quiet way, as he went to bed that night and drove the cattle back and forth from their pasture during the next few days. He was thinking of it as he walked along the sea-shore about a week later. His father was not with him this time, having gone to a city several miles away to spend the night with a sick friend."

As Mr. Percival reached this point in his story, a gust of wind arose that made the old house creak and tremble in every joint; floods of rain dashed against the little window, and the smoke at intervals puffed from the fireplace out into the room.

"There had been a long storm, and to-night the waves were running enormously large — larger than Hans had ever seen them. It was flood tide; and as they rolled up, one by one, like long green hills, they would topple over and break with a sound like thunder, so near that the spray flew all over Hans and soaked him through before he had been there two minutes. He was plodding along, with head bent down against the wind, when all at once his heart stood still, and he could almost feel his hair start up in terror at what he saw. If you had seen it, perhaps you wouldn't have noticed it; but he knew what it meant. It was a very, very small stream of water trickling out through the soil and gravel on the *inside* of the dyke. Hans knew it was the sea, which had at last found its way through. 'Before morning,' his father had said! Hans thought one moment of the awful scene that was coming, and the picture of his own home, surrounded by the terrible waves, rose before him.

"He threw himself flat upon the dyke, and thrusting the forefinger of his right hand into the hole, shrieked for help.

"It was growing dark. Hans' sister Gretchen was at that very moment crossing a moor near their house, searching and calling anxiously for him."

"Why didn't he put a rock or a stick of wood in?" demanded Kittie eagerly.

"There was no wood handy, I suppose; and even if there had been, the water would have soon forced it out of the hole. A pebble would have been useless for the same reason. No, the boy must hold the ocean with his one little hand — the wind pushing, the moon pulling against him.

"'Help! help! The dyke is breaking!'

"Nobody came. The night-fogs began to creep up from the sea, the wind shifted back to the old stormy quarter and blew hard toward the land. The tide was still rising, and the 'white cows' outside bellowed more and more terribly. The stars went out, one by one.

"'Help!'" Hans felt his finger, his hand, his whole arm, beginning to ache from the strained position, but he did not dare to change. Would nobody come?

"Blacker and blacker grew the night. The awful booming of the sea drowned entirely the now feeble cry of the boy. The leak was stopped: but could he bear it much longer? The pain shot up and down his arm and shoulder like fire-flashes, until he groaned and cried aloud. He said his prayers, partly for somebody to come and partly for strength to hold out till they did.

"The temptation came to him powerfully to take out his aching hand and run away. Nobody would know of it; and the pain was so keen! But he said his little Dutch prayers the harder, and — held on.

. . . .

"In the early gray of the morning a party of men came clambering along the dyke, shouting and swinging lanterns. At last one of them — can you guess which? — espied what looked like a heap of rags lying on the ground.

"'It's his clothes!' he cried, in a trembling

voice. Then, 'It's Hans himself, thank God! thank God!'

"He had 'held on,' you see, until he fainted with pain and exhaustion. Wet through, cold as ice, his whole hand and arm swelled terribly, he still held on, unconsciously, with his finger in the leak.

"So Hans prevented the destruction of the great dyke. He lost his own right hand in doing it, to be sure; but in losing that he had saved Holland."

"One more! One more!" chorused the children, as their uncle concluded. "That was so short!"

"Well," said he, good-naturedly, "throw on a few more 'silver rags', Tom; there's just time for a very short one before dinner. Do you remember that little Fred Colebrook who came here for a few minutes, the day the Indians were tried?"

"The one with the curly hair? Yes, sir. He's visiting at Mr. Thompson's, isn't he?"

"Yes; his home is in a queer place — at least, what was his home till last year, when his folks moved to the city.

"It was a little valley, with huge mountains on every side, so steep and so close together that you would think there was no way to get through to the world outside. Some of the mountains were covered with pine and spruce trees, clinging to their sides like the shaggy fur of a Newfoundland dog; others were bare from top to bottom, with bits of red stone tumbling over their ugly-looking ledges almost every day. The valley itself was pretty enough, with its tiny green meadow, and a brook which laughed and played in the sunshine all day long. It was rather a lonesome place, to be sure, but Fred did not mind that; for did he not have his father, and his mother, and the workingman for company; besides the old red cow, the horses, and five small gray kittens? These kittens were Fred's special pets. He was never tired of feeling their soft fur and cool little feet against his cheek, and hearing their sleepy *purr-r-purr-r*. Sometimes he would carry one of them slyly up to the sober cow, feeding quietly in front of the house, and place the kitten on her back. It was hard to tell which was more astonished, the kitten or the cow. At any rate, they both would jump, with such funny looks of surprise, and the kitten would run away as fast as ever she could, to tell her adventure to the other four.

"One warm afternoon in June, Fred was sitting on the piazza watching the kittens, as they tumbled about after their own tails, scampered across the green, or hunted grasshoppers from spot to spot. The breeze blew softly, and there was no sound in the air but the rush of the brook, just below the hill.

"The kittens raced about harder than ever. One of them in particular, whose name was Mischief, was more active than all the rest. She would jump up into the air, turn somersaults, and finally took several steps on her hind paws in her eagerness to catch a bright red butterfly, just over her head. All this amused Fred greatly as he sat there in the warm sunlight, with his head leaning against the door-post. But Mischief still kept on, becoming more and more daring. She seemed to have fairly learned to keep her balance on two feet, with the aid of her bushy tail, for she ran about, to and fro, with her fore-paws stretched out after the butterfly, like a child. Once or twice she laughed aloud. It did not seem so strange, when she was standing up in that fashion, nor was Fred at all surprised to notice that she seemed much larger than ever before.

"'Of course,' he thought, 'one is taller standing up than when one is on one's hands and knees.' The other kittens had by this time disappeared entirely from sight, leaving only Mischief, who now walked about more slowly, and, having caught the butterfly, came sauntering up to where Fred was sitting.

"'Mischief,' he began severely, 'you've no right to treat that poor butterfly '— Here he stopped, rather puzzled; what she held in her hand was certainly no butterfly; it was a fan, covered with soft black and scarlet feathers, and richly ornamented with gems.

"'Well,' said the kitten, carelessly, 'go on. You were saying it was nothing but-a-fly, I think;' and she stooped slightly to arrange the folds of her dress. This was of delicate gray velvet, fitting closely to her pretty figure and trailing on the grass behind her. Indeed, Fred now saw that she was not a kitten at all, but a dainty little lady, about as high as his shoulder. She watched him with an amused smile, and continued to fan herself. 'I had such a run for this fan,' she went on, as if to put the boy at his ease; 'the wind blew it quite out of my hand, and — dear me, there it goes again!'

"As she was speaking, the fan made a queer sort of flutter in her hands, and floated off into the sunshine. She sprang lightly into the air, whirled around after it until Fred's head was giddy, then walked back quietly and stood before him again, fanning herself slowly, as if nothing had happened.

"Fred felt that to be polite he ought to say something.

"'I don't understand, Miss —— Miss ——' he paused doubtfully.

"'That's right; Mischief,' she said promptly. 'You needn't trouble yourself to name me over again.'

"'But you're not Mischief,' persisted Fred. 'At least not the one I know. She's a kitten.'

"'Well, what am I, pray?' Fred rubbed his eyes; there she stood, looking almost exactly as she had a minute before; yet that was certainly a a fuzzy gray tail resting on the grass, and these were certainly his kitten's paws and round eyes. She was purring softly.

"'Now, Mischief,' he cried out eagerly, 'you've been playing tricks, and I'm going to stroke you the wrong way, to pay up for it.'

"The kitten stopped purring. 'Don't,' she said, sharply; 'you'll crumple my dress! There,' she added, in a gentler tone, seeing his dismay, 'you didn't mean any harm. Be a good boy and I'll let you take a walk with me.' She threw away her fan, and held out her little gloved hand to him, as she spoke, for she was a lady again beyond all doubt. Fred took her hand with some hesitation, and off they started together. As they walked along, side by side, Mischief kept up such a steady, soft little flow of talk that Fred could not tell it from purring half the time. At last they reached the foot of one of the high mountains, and Mischief began to scramble up, pulling him along as she did so.

"'But I — never — was here before,' he tried to say, as his little guide leaped from rock to stump, catching them gracefully, and swinging him up after her. Mischief never stopped, however, until they reached the very tip-top. Then they sat down to rest on a mossy rock. The view was glorious; Fred could see his house, nestling in the valley far, far below him, and looking no bigger than a pin in a green pincushion.

"'Speaking of pins,' said Mischief, as if she read

his thoughts, 'how many pine needles are there in a bunch? I suppose you learned that at school.'

"'No,' said Fred, 'we had how many shillings there are in a guinea, and how many rods make a furlong, and —' Here Mischief appeared so intensely interested that he was quite confused, and stopped short.

"'Go on,' she cried, impatiently; 'how do you make your fur long?'

"Fred was dreadfully puzzled. 'Excuse me,' he said, 'I don't think you quite understood me.'

"'Well, never mind. How about the needles?'

"'I never learned that table.'

"'Humph! I thought everybody knew there were three in a bunch on a pitch pine, and five in a bunch on a white pine. It's in the catechism.'

"'No, it's not,' said Fred, decidedly.

"'It ought to be, then, which is precisely the same thing with us kittens.'

"'It isn't with folks,' said Fred.

"'Well, let me see if you know anything at all. Do you see that black cloud coming up over the hills?'

"'Yes'm.'

"'Probably it will rain to-night, will it not?'

"'Yes'm,' replied Fred again, meekly.

"'Why should it?'

"Fred looked at the cloud blankly; he really had never thought of this before.

"'Of course you don't know,' said Mischief, after waiting a moment for him to answer. 'It's because every drop of water in that cloud has thin, gauzy wings of fog, and when they happen to come across a cold breeze — as they often do in these high mountains — they shiver and fold up their wings so they can't fly any more, and down they come in what you call a rain storm. I knew that before I had my eyes open. Now,' she continued, 'I'm going to try you just once more, and then we must be going. Did you ever see a kitten walk on tip-toes?'

"'Never,' said Fred. 'Except,' he added slyly, 'when they jump after butterflies.'

"Mischief laughed outright. 'Dear me, you funny boy,' she said, 'where *have* you been to school? Why, *all* kittens walk on tiptoes, from morning till night. That little crook that looks like a knee is really a kitten's heel. Horses walk the same way, only they have just one toe to walk on, and that longer then your arm. You ask that little gray-bearded man with the blue spectacles, that comes here once in a while, and he will tell you that many thousand years ago horses had as many toes as kittens, but they are such great, awkward things that all their other toes have been taken away from them. A cow has —'

"'I know!' cried Fred. 'She has a cloven hoof, without any toes at all.'

"'You're all wrong, as usual,' said Mischief briskly; 'what you call hoof is her two toes. Though why she should be allowed to keep more than a horse, I never could see. Great red thing!' Just then, a big drop of rain came down, spat! on Mischief's nose. She rubbed it off hastily with her nice little mouse-gray gloves, and looked about her with a frightened air. 'It never will do for me to be caught in a shower,' she said, 'or my gloves and dress will be spotted. They've been in the family a long time and were imported from Malta.' Another drop struck her face, tickling her so that she sneezed violently.

"'Come!' she cried, and started off at a full run, down the mountain-side, pulling Fred after her as before. 'Hurry, hurry,' she screamed; 'faster, faster!'

"Fred now saw, to his horror, that instead of descending the side on which they had come up, she was making straight toward the slope where the rocks were bare and red.

"'Stop, stop, Mischief!' he cried breathlessly, 'we shall go over the cliff!'

"Before the words were fairly out of his mouth they were on the crumbling edge of a precipice. In that instant Fred could see the road and the brook a thousand feet below them.

He braced his feet against the stones and tried to snatch his hand away, but Mischief held it more tightly than ever. With one wild bound they were over the brink, out in the empty air, falling down, down —

"Come, come, Fred, you'll be wet through!"

"Fred looked about him in amazement. He was sitting on the piazza, and there was Mischief in his lap. She was shaking off the rain-drops as they fell thickly upon her soft fur, and was struggling to get away from his hand, which was tightly clasped about one of her fore-paws. His other hand was held by his mother, who stood over him, laughing and talking at the same time. 'Why, Fred, have you been here all the afternoon? I

guess the kitten has had a nice nap; and just see how it rains!'

"'Mischief,' began Fred solemnly, letting go her paw, 'what have you been —?' but Mischief had already jumped and run off to the barn, to find her brothers and sisters."

CHAPTER VII.

OAK LEAVES AND HAY.

How it did pour that afternoon! It was of no use to think of going into the woods for leaves, and the girls had just about given up all idea of decorating Pet's room, when the kitchen window was obscured by a queer object.

Kittie came flying out from the sitting room, closely followed by the rest.

"What can it be?" she cried. "O, I know! It's Ruel — just see what he's brought!"

Sure enough, the kindly trapper, who loved the young folks almost as if they were his own children, had tramped off quietly to the wood, gathered a huge armful of green oak boughs — and now stood, beaming out of the midst of them, like a good-natured Faun, fairly dripping from head to foot.

"I thought you mout like to be workin' while your uncle was tellin' stories," he called out. "Where'll you have em?"

"O, in the barn, the barn. We've been cooped up in the house all day, and I'm just longing for a breath of fresh air."

Thus the energetic Bess.

"But the leaves are all wet," objected Kittie. "Won't they hurt the hay, Uncle?"

Mr. Percival smiled, and patted the eager brown head. "I guess they won't spoil the whole mow," he said. "But of course I can't tell you any stories, because I'm going to toast my feet all the afternoon in the Den."

Kittie saw a twinkle in his eye.

"Ah," she said coaxingly, "you're just teasing us. You're going to come out where you can see to Tim and Ruel while they work, and then you're going to climb up into the hay-mow and *tell*, while we make trimming — aren't you, Uncle?"

"'*Aren't* you, Uncle?'" repeated Mr. Percival in a whimsical tone. "Why, if you're such a very earnest little puss about it, I suppose — I must!"

It didn't take long to prepare for the barn. Hooded and water-proofed, the girls ran across the little open space as fast as they could go, wagging in and out under a big umbrella, screaming and laughing, girl-fashion.

Tom and Randolph followed in more military style, double-quicking in fine order from porch to barn. The men were already there. In one of the broad bays on the ground level of the barn was a mow of new hay; and on the centre of this was deposited a huge heap of leaves, wet and shining, pretty material for busy fingers to transform into links and wreaths and festoons for Pet's chamber.

Mr. Percival was soon made comfortable in a hay-nest especially hollowed out for him, and the rest seated themselves in a semi-circle before him. The boys were set to work at once, stripping off leaves.

"There," said Bess, beginning to turn the stout stems and piercing the tough green tissue of the leaves, "this is really —"

"Nice," furnished Randolph gravely. "That's a good Boston word. Girls always say that the weather is nice, and ice cream is nice, and going to Europe is nice, and the sermon was nice, and —"

"O hear him, hear him!" interrupted Kittie. "I guess 'nice' is as good a word as 'jolly.' Boys all say that."

"Many a nice time, yes, and jolly too," said

uncle Will, as he watched the swallows overhead, and listened with an amused smile to the children's funning, " I've had in this barn, in old times."

" Were there many fellows about here ? " asked Tom.

" Not many, but perhaps we appreciated one another all the better. The district school was about a half a mile from the cross-roads, and we boys were always ready for a good time. Once, though, our sport came near turning out pretty seriously for me."

" How was that, sir ? " The rest looked up with interested faces, but kept on with their work.

" Why, it was on a Saturday afternoon, I remember, at about this time of year — no, it must have been later — in August, I think.

" There were seven of us, just out of school, and ready for anything in the shape of fun. It had been a clear race from the schoolhouse — we never could go anywhere without a run or a leap-frog, or something of the sort — till we reached the shade of an apple-tree, laughing, panting and eating apples. The ground was covered with small, juicy fruit, mellow on the upper side, and hard underneath. They were pretty sour, but we didn't care.

"It was only half-past four, and we had two good hours before supper-time all to ourselves. So we lay there, filling our pockets with apples after we had eaten enough, and began to propose plans.

"'Let's go down to the mill and see 'em saw logs.'

"'Too far.'

"Well, who says 'I spy,' then?"

"This suggestion was well received, and I, who had made it, proceeded to count off, one dropping away every time until the last, who happened to be Bob Andrews — poor fellow, he was shot at Antietam! — was 'It,' and was posted against the tree with his eyes covered.

"'Fifteen, twenty, twenty-five, thirty — I'm comin' when I get to three hundred!' he shouted, as we scattered in all directions.

"At first I made for a low wall near the house, and had hardly time to gain it when Bob gave a flourish, and with a loud 'Three hundred — comin'!' started for his prey.

"Peeping through a crevice in the wall, and finding he was coming in my direction, I hurriedly glanced about for a new hiding-place.

"At that moment a red squirrel bounded lightly

along the tops of the stones, and disappeared in a crevice between two boards of the barn.

"Instantly I followed the hint. Creeping on my hands and knees, I soon reached the corner of the old gray building, and a moment later was in the centre of the mow, burrowing down out of sight, until I was pretty confident that it would take a smarter boy than Bob Andrews to find me that time.

"It was remarkably comfortable in that mow. The hay was fresh on top, and although I had reached the under layer of last year's crop, I took care not to disturb it much, so that the dust did not trouble me. I could hear the shouts of the boys as they were discovered, one after the other, and the complaining tones of Bob, who, to my great satisfaction, was ransacking every nook and corner of the place except the right one.

"A couple of swallows flew in and out over my head, twittering softly. Perhaps they were returning for a last look at their old home, for it was almost time they were away.

"Whether it was the soft August air, or the distant, faint shouts of the boys, or the voice of the swallows, I never knew; but when I roused myself to climb down and have my laugh at the rest of the fellows, to my surprise I found it was quite dark. At the same time I began to experience a smothering sensation, and an almost unbearable heat.

"I put up my hand. It instantly came into contact with hay so dry that it made me sneeze.

"I tried to push it aside and to rise; but, to my dismay, found myself held down tightly by an immovable mass above, below, on all sides. I had at first supposed the hay had tumbled or been thrown down for fun upon me; but all in a flash, I realized the truth. I had fallen asleep, and while unconscious, had been covered by some of the farm-hands, who, I remembered, had been directed that very morning to pitch the entire contents of another mow upon this, as the flooring of the first needed repairs.

"I was sixteen, then, and pretty rugged for a boy of my years; but I confess I felt a lump in my throat and a faint, dizzy terror sweep over me from head to foot.

"Buried alive in a hay-mow! For a few minutes I was quite frantic. I shrieked for help; I dug furiously with hands and kicked with feet, until my smarting eyes, nostrils and throat, half-choked with fine hay-dust, compelled me to desist.

"Then I began to plan more deliberately. It was pitch-dark, remember, and so close that I could hardly breathe. The perspiration, too, was streaming from every pore. If I had known my points of compass, I could have made a bee-line for the nearest limit of the mow, but I had turned in sleeping, and struggled so violently afterward, that I was as completely lost as though I had been in the Maine wilderness.

"There was no time to spare. My breath came in a quick, heavy panting. I felt my strength growing plainly less. At the same time, I began to be hungry and thirsty. How much time had elapsed since I had hidden away I could not tell. Perhaps it was supper-time.

"What would I have given to have been sitting in the smooth-floored, old kitchen, with my bowl of bread and milk before me, relating my strange adventure to the half-sympathizing, half-laughing faces around the table?

"I began slowly to loosen the hay upon my right side, which I judged was toward the centre of the barn. If so, my course would bring me out through the side of the mow, twenty feet above the floor.

"It was tedious work, for I dared not hurry lest I should be overcome with heat and the dust, which kept me coughing almost incessantly.

"Handful after handful I pulled out and crowded behind me. Every muscle ached with the cramped position, and the air became more and more close. Still, I worked on steadily, desperately. How long it was I cannot tell — I never knew.

"I was drawing away the tightly-packed masses of hay, a small bunch at a time, when the air suddenly became perceptibly cooler and sweeter. I dug at the cruel hay wall more furiously. Somewhere beneath me I heard a slight scrambling and rustling, which soon ceased.

"A moment later, my finger-ends struck the rough surface of boards, and, as they did so, a cold, delicious draught of air, like spring-water in a desert, blew upon my hot cheek.

"I felt about eagerly, still seeing nothing, and soon came upon a small hole or interstice, with roughened sides, as if gnawed by some animal, between the edges of two of the boards which formed the partition I had met. It did not take me long, country boy as I was, to reason out the nature of that opening. It was a squirrel's hole, without doubt the very spot where my bushy-tailed guide had disappeared, as I watched him from behind the stone wall.

"I put my eye to the opening, and looked out. To my astonishment, the stars were shining brightly. Yes, and the moon! By its position in the eastern sky — for it was past the full — I knew at last how long I had been in that hay-mow. It was between twelve and one o'clock, and for eight hours I had been buried, lost, in the hay.

"I say had been, for now I felt quite at ease. No more exploring for me that night! When morning came, I could easily call through my squirrel's front-door, and the men who came out early to milk would pitch off the hay, and release me.

"The only trouble was hunger and thirst, which, now that I had time to think of them, oppressed me more than ever. Then I remembered those apples. I suppose nothing will ever taste so good as that sour, hard apple did that night. After I had made a bountiful lunch, I enlarged my quarters a little, settled back comfortably, and waited for milking-time.

"That's all there really is to tell. In due time, the stars faded, one by one; the sky flushed all sorts of lovely roses and pinks; the cattle began to stir about uneasily underneath; a distant door creaked, and heavy boots slowly approached.

"I placed my lips to the crack, and called in a low tone. You see, I didn't want to rouse all the folks. I knew they wouldn't be worried, because I had planned to go over to Merritt's and stop with him that very night.

"Well, ten minutes later I stood on the barn-floor, brushing the hay-seed from my hair and clothes, and stretching my aching limbs. I found the witch-grass had cut my fingers a little, and that was about all the harm that came of it.

"I expected them all to laugh at the breakfast-table, and told my story rather sheepishly; but when I got through, and looked round, the folks had anything but smiling faces, and two of them passed me the doughnuts, both at once. Mother cried outright.

"If he hadn't taken the right direction,' she said, 'or had kept going in a circle' —

"Then she stopped; and so will I."

"Ah," said Kittie, drawing a long breath, "that

was a narrow escape. It makes me feel stifled just to think of it."

"Was it this very barn, Uncle?"

"Yes, Tom; and that further mow on the other side, where Kittie found the man last winter, and had such a fright."

The trimming was nearly completed, but it still needed to be brought into better shape, and a special yard or two of smaller leaves made for the looking-glass, Bess said. "And can't you tell us one more hay-mow story, uncle Will."

"Let me speak to Tim a minute," said Mr. Percival. "After I've given him some directions, I'll see if I can remember one.

"It was a warm day in the early part of April," he began, as soon as he returned. "The air was mild, the sky was blue, with sunlight, and the gentle spring breezes were full of all sorts of nice smells of fresh earth and green, growing turf. The turf was in the moist places on the sunny side of the old wall; above it, in their willow-baskets, pussies were beginning to stretch out their little gray paws sleepily, as they awoke one by one from their long nap.

"As Zip spattered along the muddy road-side on

his way home from Sunday-school, he thought the world a pretty nice place to live in, on the whole. 'Zip,' by the way, was short for 'Zephaniah,' which was his long name. Folks only called him that when they were full of fun or very cross; indeed, you could generally tell which by their tone.

"A robin in the overhanging boughs of an apple-tree whistled cheerily as Zip drew near. Instantly the boy seized a stone, and threw it at the red feathers. The bird uttered a shrill cry of alarm, but flew away unharmed, and presently was heard again far away in the orchard. Zip was rather glad of this, after all. He wasn't a cruel boy, but whenever he saw a bird or a squirrel, something in him, he couldn't tell what, made him throw stones at it.

"Now Zip, as I said, had just been to Sunday-school, and had been thinking almost all the way home of the lesson. It was the story of the very first Christian people, who started so bravely to be good and true, and who tried to do just as Christ of Nazareth had taught them and their fathers a few years before.

"'What a beautiful world it would be,' the

teacher had said, at the close of school, 'if everybody tried to do so now!'

"Zip was only twelve years old, and didn't know much about the world any way, but he had seen some acts that were quite unlike those of the apostles so long ago. His father and mother were plain country people, working hard from morning till night, and giving no anxious thought to the morrow, but a great deal to to-day, which was pretty much the same thing, only they were one day behind, and somehow could never catch up. The hard-featured man at the counter of his country store, and the tired-looking woman in the kitchen, each spent their lives, it seemed to Zip, in getting dinner or clearing it away. So it happened that the boy was glad enough of his Sunday afternoon, when, after returning from school, he had three hours to himself before supper.

"As he neared home he saw the small cattle-door of the barn left invitingly open. He turned aside, picking his way among the brown pools and streamlets that dimpled and twinkled in the sunlight, and entered the great fragrant cave, lighted only by cracks between the uneven boards, and a knot-hole here and there far above his head. The oxen raised their broad foreheads, knocking their horns against the stanchions. Zip gave them each a little pat between their meek brown eyes, and scrambled up the ladder into the hay-mow.

It was a delicious place for a quiet Sunday afternoon. He waded over to the very centre of the mow, dug a little hollow with his hands, and cuddled down into it. Over his head were the dark beams with their dusty webs and last year's swallow's nests; beneath him he could hear the cattle munching away at their hay and grain, and now and then putting down a heavy foot on the floor of their stalls. A dozen hens were stalking about, picking wisely at various bits of grass-seed, and clucking in soft tones. All around was the sweet scent of the hay.

"As Zip lay in his snug nest he thought drowsily of what the teacher had said about everybody being good. How comfortable and happy it would be! The more he thought about it the pleasanter it seemed. Just then there came a long, low note from one of the hens on the wide floor below. The sound had so many quirks and turns in it, that Zip half thought for a moment that it was some one speaking to him, and started up to answer. Then he remembered it was only a hen, and leaned back with a smile.

Presently he heard the same hen clucking, or cackling, again, and so slowly and clearly did the notes come that he could have stated to a positive certainty that something had been said down there on the barn floor, and that, too, about himself. He crept to the edge of the mow and looked over. There were the hens just as he had often seen them, only looking wiser than ever. Even while he looked the brown pullet gave a vigorous scratch or two, pecked at the dusty boards once or twice, shook her feathers, and said distinctly,

"'If they only knew!'

"Zip stared. Then a deep, soft voice, hardly more than a long, long sigh, came from directly beneath him, 'They would soon learn to be as quiet as we are.'

"It was Star, the off-ox; there couldn't be a doubt of it.

"'I don't know,' answered the brown pullet, winking upside down after her custom, "you great things are almost too quiet. One has to be lively to get one's supper, you know.'

"As she spoke she made a quick run after a tiny

insect which had been called out of its cranny by the warm sun, caught it on the wing, and went on with what she had been saying.

"' In the first place, Star,' she said, more gravely, ' no one would be angry without good reason, and then they wouldn't beat animals for nothing, would they, Billy ? '

" The horse who was thus addressed seemed to shake his mane, and said something which Zip took to be a very prolonged ' nay,' but he wasn't quite sure he answered at all.

"' Nobody would be selfish, and everybody would be kind,' continued Brown Pullet, 'and trying to please others instead of themselves. They wouldn't hurt the feelings of anybody nor anything. There's Zip, now, he wouldn't throw stones at a robin ; he would think how the poor little bird-heart was beating faster and faster, and the soft red feathers throbbing on her breast, as the ugly stone came whizzing through the air to take her life ! '

" Zip did think, and was sorry he threw the stone. It was a comfort that he didn't hit the bird, however, and he made up his mind to throw out some crumbs on the well-curb that very night.

"HE WAS OFTEN AWAY FROM THE HOUSE, ALONE."

"'I declare,' said Brown Pullet, with her feathers just a bit ruffled, 'when I think of how pleasant and kind and polite and gentle folks might be, and how they do say sharp, hurtful things (which I've heard people say do bruise one more even than rocks), it makes me really — there!' she interrupted herself, 'I declare, I'm getting angry myself, which don't help matters much. The best way for me to bring on the good times is to begin myself. Speckle, Speckle,' she called to one of her companions, 'here's the plumpest barleycorn I've found to-day. I sha'n't have any peace till I see you eat it, to make up for my being cross to you this morning when you tipped the water over on my toes. It was cold, to be sure, but 'twas all an accident, and I oughtn't to have pecked you for it. Dear, dear, how late it's getting! It's quite dark, da-a-rk, da-r-r-rk!'

"Zip gave a little jump, he hardly knew why, and looked about him. The hens were still walking about the floor below, for he heard them as plainly as before, only he couldn't seem to make out what they said, and somehow, too, he was back in his soft hay-nest again. He rubbed his eyes, and stretched his sturdy little arms, found his way down the ladder, and looked hard at the brown pullet. But she merely clucked in her old way, and, turning her head on one side, looked up at him curiously out of her wise, round eyes.

"Zip then went over to see the two oxen, but they only lifted their heads and watched him in silence for a moment, then gave two great, soft, sweet-breathed sighs, and went on eating their hay."

The oak-leaf decorations were now quite finished. The remainder of the day, until dark, was spent in festooning them about Pet's room, over the doorways, and even in the chamber to be occupied by poor little Bridget Flanagan, the unrecognized heroine of the Summer Street fire.

Ruel, coming in to supper, reported bright streaks in the west, and predicted fair cool weather on the morrow.

CHAPTER VIII.

POOR TOM!

THAT Ruel was a good weather-prophet, there could be no doubt. Long before blue eyes and brown were opened at The Pines, the sun was shining over hill and valley, and birds singing in every thicket, to welcome the bright day.

Plans were eagerly discussed at breakfast, and by eight o'clock the great wagon was before the door, ready for a start. Tom alone hung back and refused to go, saying he wanted to walk over to the Pond; so they drove off without him, toward the Pineville Station.

The horses, who had just enjoyed a rainy day's rest in their stalls, stepped off merrily. How sweet the air was! The girls and Randolph drew in long breaths, and shouted and sang till they were tired. Mr. Percival listened, and watched them with kindly eyes, now and then engaging in the conversation himself.

"Aren't there any boys and girls around here except ourselves?" asked Randolph as they whirled along over the road, here carpeted with pine needles.

"O there are plenty in Readville and Jamestown," replied his uncle, touching the glossy flank of the off horse with his whip. "There's a good-sized school in each town, and they draw the young folks together, from all parts."

"What do they do for fun, I wonder?"

"Well, just now they're full of base ball. The boys do the hard work, out in the sun, and the girls make caps and badges for them and watch them play. There's a club in each town, I'm told."

"How nice!" exclaimed Bess. "I do so like to see real exciting games!"

"Don't you believe we could drive over some time, Uncle?" asked Kittie.

"Yes indeed, yes indeed; take you over to-morrow if you like — or send you with Ruel."

"They'd be glad enough to git the boys to play with 'em," remarked Ruel, chiming in as his name was spoken. "They always think city boys must know how, because they've seen the big clubs"

It might as well be added right here that the

boys did go over to Readville, though not on the following day; and the village club were so well pleased with their playing, that they invited the new-comers to join their nine, during vacation, and to take part in any matches that might occur. Randolph, indeed, so gained in favor by his pleasant ways and cool head that he was regularly elected Captain. Tom did well, too, being a more graceful player than his cousin, but not so reliable in an emergency. All this I have mentioned, to explain how the great Match Game came about, of which we shall hear before long.

Meanwhile the ride to the railroad progressed pleasantly. An excursion to Bessie's mountain (where she had lighted the birch-tree torch during the thunder-storm) was planned in all its details.

"Pet will soon be rested," said Kittie in gleeful tones, "and then we'll have our picnic. Ruel, you must take plenty of matches, and your axe."

"What's the axe fer?"

"O tables, and a tent, perhaps."

"And birch bark," added the guide.

"Birch bark? I thought you cut that off with penknives. O, can we get a lot, to carry home?"

"Don't see why not, ef you c'n stan' the work."

"Has Pet another watch?" asked Randolph suddenly. "She said something about it in her last letter to you, Bess, didn't she?"

"No. Her father thinks it was careless of her to lose it, now that it's certain it didn't go into the pond when she fell overboard."

"I should like to know what's the matter with Tom," broke in Kittie. "He's acted queer, ever since that day."

"Yes," said Mr. Percival soberly. "I'm troubled about the boy. He isn't his old merry self at all."

"What did he say about the Indians that afternoon, Uncle?"

"Said he believed they took the watch and hid it; and that he hadn't seen it himself, and knew nothing about it."

"Was that at the trial?"

"Just before. He wasn't in the house when we examined the Indians."

"Well, he thinks everything of Pet," said Randolph. "I guess he feels bad about her losing it, and that's what ails him. "Hulloa, see that crow on the fence just ahead there!"

"He's gone, he's gone! O what are those little birds fluttering round him?"

"Them's king-birds," said Ruel. "They can't put up with crows, nohaow."

"What, are they fighting him now?"

"Teeth an' claws. Look at him dive, to git out o' their way!"

"Do crows do any good, Ruel?"

"Wal, I d'no. I s'pose, when you come right daown to it, the creeturs ought ter be killed off. They do suck small bird's eggs, an' they're a powerful nuisance in a cornfield. But thar, I do hate to shoot anything with wings on 'em, in these big woods."

"Why, Ruel?" inquired the boy curiously.

"Wal, fer one reason, they're good company, even those black rascals. Many's the time I've been off alone in the woods, in the winter, when I couldn't see nor hear a livin' thing fer a week together. An' some mornin' I'd hear a queer croakin' noise near my cabin, an' thar'd be a crow — head on one side, a-talkin' to a neighbor over 'n a pine. Their talkin' ain't anything like their reg'lar cawin'."

"What does it sound like?"

"O, I d'no. Like a hoarse old man, talkin' to himself, p'raps. Anyway, it sounds sort o' human, and I couldn't knock 'em over, to save me."

By this time the girls had found something else to interest them by the roadside, in the treetops, or the sky overhead; and so the ride went on, happily, toward Pineville.

But it is time to look back a little, and see what Tom is about, left alone at The Pines.

As soon as the rest were gone, Tom glanced carelessly over his shoulder, and sauntered off toward the woods. At a distance of about a thousand feet from the house, he paused and looked curiously about him. He had entered a clump of oaks and birches, just on the edge of the pine forest; before him lay a little valley, into which he descended, and leaving the path, followed the course of what was evidently in the spring season a small stream, now entirely dry. Stepping cautiously, to avoid treading upon dry twigs, he kept on down the ravine until he reached a large bowlder, forming the outworks of a picturesquely broken cliff whose fern-draped front towered some forty feet or more above his head.

An aged beech tree, rooted about half-way up the juncture of the boulder and the cliff, had bent down ward in the course of years, until its lowermost branches almost touched the ground. Seizing the nearest of these, and aiding himself by slight projections and crannies in the ledge itself, Tom drew himself up to the thick end of the tree, upon the curving trunk of which he seated himself, breathless. He was now in a sort of cavity, formed by the fall of the bowlder in ages past, which had given shelter to the young beech and collected soil for its nourishment. Ferns grew thickly above, below, on every side, along the shelving surfaces, which, projecting over Tom's head, made a snug nook some five or six feet deep. This hiding-place the boy flattered himself was entirely his own discovery, and thither he was accustomed to betake himself on long summer afternoons; then, stretching out comfortably at full length in the green shade, he would fancy himself in a wild country, flying from Indians; or would pull a book from his pocket, and lose himself in tales of peril and adventure.

On this occasion, however, he had no book, and gave himself up to no day dreams. Instead, he seemed worried and frightened, and peering downward through the leaves, listened for any footstep that might be approaching.

No, he was quite alone. Only a thrush, singing musically, near by; and from beyond, the solemn, never-ceasing murmur of the pines.

With slow and careful movements, taking care not to disturb the loose rocks or soil in the cavity, the boy turned and thrust his arm into a narrow cleft that had been concealed by a clump of ferns.

When he drew back his hand, something bright gleamed in it. It was round, and shone gayly in an innocent bit of sunlight that came flickering down through the tree-tops. It was talking to itself, too, in a very busy and wise little way, as Tom satisfied himself at once, holding it to his ear and listening anxiously.

What would Pet have thought, as she whirled along in the North-bound express from Boston that fair morning, could she have seen Tom crouching on the shadowy ledge, trembling at every sound in the forest, pale and frightened, clasping in his hand — her lost watch? Poor Tom!

CHAPTER IX.

A MOUNTAIN CAMP.

"I SHOULD like to know," said Pet breathlessly, as she clambered up the steep slope of Saddleback, a day or two after her return to The Pines, "whether there really is any top to this hill! Where was the birch you set on fire, Bess?"

The party paused a minute beside the path, to rest and get breath.

"O, ever so far from here, away over on the Readville side of the mountain."

"It spiles the looks of the tree," observed Ruel, leaning on his axe, "or I'd start one for ye naow. Leaves 'em all black, an' sometimes kills 'em, right aout — not to say anything 'bout settin' the rest o' the woods on fire."

"What sort of a birch is that, over by that rock, uncle Will?" asked Randolph.

"That? That's a black birch. Nice tasting bark. When we get to the top and have lunch, we'll talk about birches a little, if you like. Let me see, whose favorite tree was it last year? Tom's?"

"Bessie's, of course. Tom's was the oak, because it wore squirrels and oak-leaf trimming!"

"Anyway," said Tom, who, though a shade paler than in the old days, seemed to have partially recovered his spirits, "oak trees are stronger and tougher than pines or birches either; and I notice that uncle Will has a white oak cane, this very minute!"

"Time's up!" interrupted Ruel, who always assumed the place of guide, not to say leader, in such tramps as these. "It's eleven o'clock naow, and we've got a good piece to go yet, 'fore we're onto the top of old Saddleback."

The woods were very still, the air cool and fragrant, the moss deep and soft under their feet, as they passed onward and upward.

> Climbing, climbing,
> Climbing up Zion's hill!

sang the girls, over and over, till the rest caught the air and joined in heartily, keeping step with the music. Now they turned an abrupt corner, and from the summit of a high ledge could look far off over the valley, with its piney woods and peaceful columns of smoke rising here and there. Loon Pond glistened gayly in the full radiance of the noon sun; now they attacked a rough natural stairway of bowlders and fallen trees, the boys clambering up first, baskets on arm, and then reaching down to give the others a helping hand. Pet, who was not used to such rough travelling, had to stop and rest every few feet; but no face was sunnier or laugh merrier than hers. Tom kept as near her side as possible, and gave her many a helpful lift with his strong arm, over the worst places. At one time she suddenly remembered that she had left her handkerchief at the last halting-place; her cavalier was off before she could stop him, racing down the steep path and returning with the missing article in an incredibly short time.

Still upward. The bowlders were prettily draped with ferns, which had sunbeams given them to play with. In the underbrush close by, a flock of partridges walked demurely and fearlessly along beside the party, clucking in soft tones their surprise and curiosity. Tiny brooks crossed the path and ran off laughing down the hill. Now there arose a rushing sound, louder and more steadily continuous than the wind-dreams in the tree-tops.

It was a cataract, falling some eight feet into a black pool, covered with little floating rafts of foam. And now they could see sky between the trunks of trees ahead.

"Hurrah!" shouted Tom. "There's the top!"

But the top was a good walk from there, and when at last they emerged upon the little rocky plateau forming the summit, they were both tired and hungry.

"Rest for thirty minutes," proclaimed Mr. Percival. "Then we'll take the back track."

"The back track! Oh-h-h!"

"How about dinner, uncle?"

"I'm just *starving*, sir!"

"What time is it? Who's got a watch?"

Tom turned fiery red at this last question, and a sober look crossed Pet's face; but a moment later she was merry again.

"*Please*, uncle Will," she pleaded, "mayn't we have lunch before we go down?"

"*Please*, Miss Pet, turn one of those brooks upside-down, and bring up a few nice large birch trees — and this will be quite a comfortable spot for dinner! No, dear, we'll look all we want to at this beautiful view, and then we'll walk down a bit — only a few steps, and not just the way we came — to a spot Ruel knows of, where shade, fuel and fresh water are all at hand."

The view was indeed lovely: lakes shining here and there in the woods; far-away villages, with tiny white church spires; mossy green acres — thousands on thousands — of forest; the dim blue of Katahdin, to the northeast; overhead, the tenderest and bluest of midsummer skies.

"How beautiful that mountain looks!" said Pet slowly, from the turfy couch where she had thrown herself down. "I wonder if there are strange Indian stories and legends about it?"

"A good many, I expect," replied Mr. Percival, baring his forehead to the cool breeze. "The Indians have always had a great respect for mountains, especially where there was some peculiar formation or feature which impressed their imagination — the 'Profile,' for instance, in the White Mountains."

"I have heard the same about the Mount of the Holy Cross in Colorado," added Randolph. "That was one of the —" he paused and flushed a little, as if uncertain whether to go on.

"Yes, yes," laughed uncle Will, guessing from his manner what he was about to say. "It's that famous brother of yours again. You ought to bring him up here sometime, to recite his own verses. However, you do it very well, for him."

"What has he written about that mountain, Randolph?" asked Kittie in a respectful tone that made the rest laugh.

"O, only three or four verses," said Randolph. "You know the Cross is formed by two immense ravines near the summit of the mountain, where the ice and snow lie all the year round. These are the verses.

THE MOUNT OF THE HOLY CROSS.

Down the rocky slopes and passes
    Of the everlasting hills
Murmur low the crystal waters
    Of a thousand tiny rills;

Bearing from a lofty glacier
    To the valley far below
Health and strength to every creature, —
    'T is for them " He giveth snow."

On thy streamlet's brink the wild deer
    Prints with timid foot the moss;
To thy side the sparrow nestles, —
    Mountain of the Holy Cross!

> Pure and white amid the heavens
> God hath set His glorious sign:
> Symbol of a world's deliverance,
> Promise of a life divine.

A little pause followed the poem, which Randolph had repeated in low, quiet tones. At length it was time to go, and with Ruel for guide once more, they threaded their way over fallen trees, around stumps and treacherous ledges, down the mountain side until, at a distance of perhaps a furlong from the summit, the guide threw down his axe.

"I guess this'll dew," said he.

"This" was a small cleared spot, some fifty feet across, along the further side of which ran the brook, forming half-a-dozen mimic cataracts. The woods on all sides were composed of evergreens, interspersed with clumps of white birch showing prettily here and there among the darker shadows.

"Now," said Mr. Percival briskly, "you and the girls can start a fire and set the table, Randolph, while Tom helps Ruel and me to build a camp."

"O, a camp! Where shall we make the fire?"

"Over against that rock, on the lee side of the clearing, so the smoke sha'n't bother us."

All hands were soon at work vigorously. Ruel cut two strong, crotched uprights, and a cross-pole, which Tom carried to their position near the brook, as directed by his uncle. A frame-work was soon erected, and long, slender poles stretched from the cross-piece back to the ground. Next, Ruel took his sharp axe, and calling for the rest to follow, plunged into the woods. In two minutes they came to a halt in the midst of a group of fine birches, whose boles shone like veritable silver.

The guide raised his axe, and laying the keen edge against the bark of the nearest, as high as he could reach, drew it steadily downward. The satiny bark parted on either side at the touch, asking for fingers to pull it off. Ruel served a dozen other trees in the same way, and then all set to work, separating bark from trunk. Tom found that his was apt to split at every knot, but by watching his uncle he soon learned to work more carefully, often using his whole arm to pry off the bark instead of merely taking hold with his fingers.

In this way they soon had a lot of splendid sheets, averaging about four feet wide by five or

THE MOUNT OF THE HOLY CROSS.

six long These they rolled into three bundles, each taking one, and bore them back in triumph to the camp. They found the table set, fire crackling, and company waiting with sharpened appetites. Ruel declared, however, that he must "git the bark onto the camp afore he eat a crumb;" and the rest helping with a will, the task was soon accomplished. If Ruel had taken a quiet look at the sky, and had his own reasons for finishing the hut — he kept his forebodings to himself, and worked on in silence. The sheets of bark were laid upon the rafters, lapping over each other like shingles, while other poles were placed on top, to keep the bark in place. By the aid of stout cord, side sheets were lashed on roughly, but well enough for a temporary shelter on a summer day; and the camp was complete.

"What shall we name it?" asked Kittie.

"'Camp Ruel'!" cried Pet, clapping her hands. "Three cheers for Camp Ruel!" And they were given lustily, with many additional "tigers" and cat-calls by the boys.

After the more serious part of lunch was disposed of, the party were comfortably seated in front of the camp, on rocks and mossy trunks.

Close at hand ran the brook, talking and laughing busily to itself.

"I wish, Uncle," said Bess, taking her favorite position by his side, "you'd tell us a story about this brook. If you don't know any, you can make it up."

"I suppose," said Mr. Percival reflectively, "I could tell you about Midget. Only Midget was such a little fellow, and you boys and girls are so exceedingly mature nowadays!"

"O, do!"

"Well, Midget, you see, is an odd little fellow. He has long, light hair, which the other boys on the street would make fun of if they were not so fond of him; a rather pale face, though it is browner now, after half a summer in the country; and big blue eyes, that seem like bits of sky that baby Midget caught on his way down from heaven, ten years ago, and never lost.

"Last September, Midget was at Crawford's, in the White Mountains: and one bright morning he took a walk, all alone, in a path that runs beside a little brook leaping down the mountain-side near the hotel. Now there is this curious thing about Midget — and that's why I began by calling him

PET.

odd — namely, that when he is alone, all sorts of things about him begin to talk; at least, he says they do, with a funny twinkle and a sweet look in his blue eyes, which make me half believe that the talk he hears comes from heaven too. At any rate, Midget had a wonderful report to make of his walk that morning; and, as nearly as I can remember, this was his account:

"He said he had not gone far into the forest when he was startled, for a moment, by hearing a group of children, somewhere in the woods, all laughing and talking together, and having the merriest time possible. Through the tumult of their happy cries he could distinguish a woman's voice, so deep and musical and tender that it filled him with delight. He hurried up the path, turned the corner where he expected to find them, and behold! it was the brook itself talking and laughing.

"Every separate tiny waterfall had its own special voice, as different from the rest as could be, but all chiming together musically and joining with the grander undertone of what most people suppose to be merely a larger cataract, but which Midget plainly perceived was a tall, lovely lady, with flowing, fluttering robes of white.

"And now she was singing to him. How he listened! Her song, he says, was something like this:

> Down from the mosses that grow in the clouds
> My children come dancing and laughing in crowds;
> They dance to the valleys and meadows below,
> And make the grass greener wherever they go.

"'But they have to go always just in one place,' said Midget, addressing the waterfall Lady.

"'That's true,' said the Lady.

"'It can't be much fun,' said Midget.

"'Oh, yes!' said the Lady, merrily, letting a cool scarf of spray drift over the boy's puzzled face.

"'But I like to go wherever I like,' said Midget.

"'So do my children. They like to go wherever they're sent. They know they're doing right, so long as they do that, and doing right makes them like it.'

"'H'm,' said Midget.

"'Besides,' added the Lady, 'once in a while, in the spring, they're allowed to take a run off into the woods a bit, just for fun.'

"'I should like that,' said Midget decisively. 'But who — who sends them, ma'am?'

"'Ah!' said the Lady, softly, 'that's the best part of all. It is our Father, who loves us, and often walks beside his brooks and through the meadows.'

"As she spoke, the end of the white scarf floated out into the sunshine, and instantly glistened with fair colors. And at the same moment the Lady began to sing:

>Down from the mountain-top
> Flows the clear rill,
>Dance, little Never-stop,
> Doing His will;
>Through the dark shadow-land,
> Down from the hill,
>To the bright meadow-land,
> Doing His will,
>Loving and serving and praising Him still.

"Just then a low rumble was heard, far off on the slopes of Mt. Washington, across the valley.

"'There!' exclaimed Midget, 'I must be going. Good-by, dear Lady-fall!'

"'Good-by, good-by!' sang the brook, as Midget hurried away down the path toward the hotel.

'He arrived just in time to escape a wetting. How it did rain! The lightning glittered and the thunder rolled until the people huddled about the big fire in the parlor were fairly scared into silence.

"But Midget, with wide-open eyes, was not a bit frightened, and kept right on telling me this story."

"Ah," said Pet, "that's lovely. But I suspect it was a dear old gentleman, and not a small boy, who heard the waterfall lady sing."

"She is there, anyway," said uncle Will, "and I can show her to you at Crawford's, within two minutes' walk of the hotel, the very next time we go there."

Pet looked puzzled, but said nothing.

"Uncle," said Kittie, throwing a few strips of bark on the fire, "you said something about having a talk on birches."

"Well, dear — it must be a short one — how many kinds of birches do you suppose there are in our woods?"

"O, two — no, let me see — three. White, and Black — "

"And Yellow," put in Tom with an air of wisdom.

"And Red and Canoe," added Mr. Percival, with a smile.

"So many! What are they good for?"

"Canoes, tents and — nurses."

"Nurses!"

"The growth of birches is so rapid that they are excellent for planting beside other trees which are less hardy, so that the birches, or "nurses," as the gardeners call them, may shelter the babies from extreme heat or cold."

"How funny! I knew, of course, that a garden of young trees was called a nursery!"

"Then the real Canoe Birch, which isn't common hereabouts, was formerly much used by the Indians for canoes and wigwams."

"How did they make the pieces stay?"

"Sewed them."

"Thread?"

"The slender roots of spruces. See!" And pulling up a tiny spruce that grew by the rock on which he sat, he showed them the delicate, tough rootlets. "Then," he added, "of course the bark is very useful for kindling, in the woods. The White Birch is almost always found with or near the White Pine."

"I like to think of their being 'princes,' in 'silver rags'," said Pet. "I should think there ought to be a legend about that, among the Indians."

Something in their uncle's expression made them all shout at once, "There is! There is! O, please tell it!"

"Well, well," laughed Mr. Percival, "fortunately for all of us, it isn't very long. Tom, keep the fire going, while you listen. The rest of you may interrupt and ask questions, whenever you wish.

"A great, great many years ago, centuries before Columbus dreamed of America, the Indians say the country was ruled by a king whose like was never known before nor since. In an encampment high up on the slopes of the Rocky Mountains he lived, and held his royal court. No one knew his age, but though his beard fell in white waves over his aged breast, his eye was as bright as an eagle's and his voice strong and wise in every council of the chiefs."

"What was his name?" asked Randolph.

"He was called Manitou the Mighty. In his reign the Indian people grew prosperous and happy. So deeply did they love and revere him that it was quite as common to speak of him as 'father,' as to address him as 'king.'

"'Yes,' said the monarch, when he heard of

this, 'yes, truly they are my children. They are all princes, are they not? — my forest children!'

"So the years sped by. The king showed his age not a whit, save by his snowy locks; and peace ruled throughout the land.

"At last Manitou the Mighty called his chiefs, his 'children,' together in council.

"'I am going away,' he said, to far-off countries, perhaps never to return. But I shall know of my subjects, and shall leave them a book of laws and directions, and they shall still be my children, and I shall be their father and king.'

"Then the chiefs hid their faces and went out to the people with the sorrowful tidings. And when the next morn broke, the Manitou had vanished.

"A week passed; and now began jealousies, hatred, avarice, tumults."

"Why didn't they obey the laws in that book?" asked Kittie.

"Well, in the first place, some professed to believe that the chiefs made up the story about the book altogether, and had written the laws themselves; though a child might have known that no other than Manitou could possibly have thought and written out such glorious and gentle words as the law book contained. Others pretended to live by the book, but so twisted the meaning of its words that the result was worse than if they had openly transgressed the law.

"So matters went on, from bad to worse. Messages arrived now and then from the king, with pleading and warning words, but in vain.

"There came a day, in the dead of winter, when the chiefs met in stormy conclave. Each one would be king. 'Manitou,' cried one and another, 'called me his child, said I was a prince! Who shall rule over me!'

"The sound of a far-off avalanche, high up among the ice-fields of the mountains, interrupted the assembly. Clouds gathered, black and ominous. Rain-drops fell, hissing, upon the pine-tops and the wigwams of Manitou's wayward children. A hurricane arose, and swept away into the roaring flood of the rapidly rising river all the wealth they had been so eager to gain. The rumbling of avalanche upon avalanche grew more terrible, nearer, nearer. The people turned to fly, with one accord, but it was too late. Behold, the Manitou stood in their midst, his long white beard tossed in the storm, his terrible eyes flashing not with rage, but with grieved love.

"'Children, children!' he cried, in a voice that, with its sad and awful sweetness, broke their very hearts for shame and remorse, 'Is it thus that the princes of our race obey their father and fit themselves to rule with him in the land beyond the great waters!'

"Then the people bowed their heads and moaned and threw up their arms wildly, and swayed to and fro in the storm, and wailed, until — until —"

The girls leaned forward breathlessly. Tom forgot to heap bark upon the fire. Ruel had slipped away to the summit, some minutes before.

"Until there was no longer a prince to be seen, but only a vast assembly of writhing, tossing, quivering forest trees, the rain dropping from their trembling leaves, their branches swaying helplessly in the wind which moaned sadly through the forest. Only one trace remained of their former greatness. Their bark, unlike that of every other tree, was silvery white, and hung in tatters about them — as you have seen them to-day, along this mountain side. For since that hour the beggared princes have wandered far and wide, still wearing their silver rags, still weeping and moaning when the storms are at their highest, and they recall that awful day."

Pet drew a long breath. "And Manitou, what became of him?"

"He still reigns, the legend goes, in the bright land beyond the great waters."

"And must the princes always be birches?"

"Ah, Pet, that is the most beautiful part of the tradition. By patient continuance in well-doing, by self-sacrifice, by living for others, the poor trees may at last make themselves worthy to see the king once more as his children, leaving the withered tree-house behind. But not until life is done, and well done.

"So you see, every white birch is eager to give its bark for fuel and protection, which is nearly all it can do, save to watch over the young trees of the forest, as I have told you, to shield them from harm.

"It is a long time for a birch to wait, sometimes many, many years before even a little child will strip off one of its tattered shreds and laugh for delight at the pretty bit of silver in its hand, little dreaming of the prince whose garment it is;

but the tree quivers with joy at the thought that it has made one of these little ones happy for even a moment, for so it has become more worthy to meet the king."

As Mr. Percival finished, Ruel returned from the summit of Saddleback.

"You'd better get the things into camp, and foller 'em yourselves. There's a storm comin'. The wind's jest haowlin', over in the birches on the west side of the maounting."

CHAPTER X.

THE STORM.

IT was fortunate that Ruel made that little exploring expedition, all by himself, for the storm was evidently rising fast. The sun went out; clouds rolled up over the western sky until it seemed as if evening were coming on; the forest was perfectly silent, except for a troubled rustling of the birches, the plash of the brook, and a dull, far-off sound like the waves of a distant ocean.

Mr. Percival drove all the party into the camp, and Ruel busied himself in laying on extra poles and closing every crack where the rain might beat in at the sides.

Kittie and Bess had been out in a storm before with their uncle, so they didn't much mind it. Pet nestled up close beside them, and waited with wide open eyes, hardly knowing whether to be more frightened or delighted at the prospect. Tom was by far the most nervous of the party, fidgeting about, begging Ruel to come inside, and behaving so queerly that Bess declared with a laugh that she believed he felt like the princes, when the Manitou was coming. As she spoke there was an ominous and prolonged roll of thunder, and the tree-tops bent under the first rush of the on-coming tempest.

Tom started and turned white to the very lips, but answered never a word.

"Don't bother the boy," said Mr. Percival kindly. "See — the storm is really upon us now!"

A glittering flash of lightning accompanied his words, and was followed by a rattling discharge of thunder. Up to this time, not a drop of rain had fallen, but now it began to patter like bullets on the dry leaves, the fire, and, loudest of all, on the bark roof above them.

Ruel crept in at last, and all seven curled up in as small compass, as far from the half-open front, as possible. How it did pour! It came down in torrents, in sheets, with an uninterrupted roar.

"Fire's gittin' tired," remarked Ruel, after about two minutes of this; and sure enough, nothing was left but a few charred brands, steaming sulkily.

The lightning and thunder now came almost simultaneously, flashing and booming until the very sky above them seemed ablaze.

After a few attempts at conversation the young folks gave it up, and remained silent. Pet was very much frightened and hid her face on Kittie's shoulder, giving a little involuntary cry whenever an unusually loud peal of thunder crashed overhead.

For a full half-hour the fury of the storm lasted. Then it rolled away over the hills and left only a light rain falling. It was still far too wet for them to leave their shelter, but the party recovered their spirits, and Ruel even managed to coax a new fire to blaze on the ruins of the old, with the aid of some dry bark and sticks he had prudently stowed away at the first alarm. The cheerful blaze and hissing crackle of the fire were reassuring, and voices soon rose again, as merrily as ever.

"What time do you s'pose it is?"

"Three o'clock!"

"Say, aren't you *awfully* stiff? Do let me move my foot a little!"

"Kit, let's have a song. That one about the pines." This was from Tom.

Kittie accordingly sang the following lines, to a bright little air. They were written by Randolph's brother, she admitted with a blush and a laugh; the tune was in Whiting's Third Music Reader:

> The pines have gathered upon the hill,
>   To watch for the old-new moon;
> I hear them whispering — "Hush, be still,
>   It is coming, coming soon;
>   Coming, coming soon!"
>
> The brown thrush sings to his small brown wife
>   Who broods below on her nest,
> "Of all the wide world and of all my life,
>   It is you I love the best,
>   You I love the best!"
>
> But the baby moon is wide awake,
>   And its eyes are shining bright;
> The pines in their arms the moon must take
>   And rock him to sleep to-night,
>   Rock him to sleep to-night!

Kittie's voice was a soft contralto, and though not strong, was very sweet. There were hand-clapping and thanks in profusion; then a unanimous cry for a story — something about a thunder-shower.

These young people, be it said, always called on their uncle Will for a story upon any subject, with as much confidence as you would have in ordering roast beef or cake at a hotel, without looking at the bill.

"Very well," said the story-teller, after a moment's reflection, "I'll tell you about Patsy's Prayer."

"It was a sultry afternoon in August. In the government offices, from the Alleghanies to Eastport, men were busily making up weather reports of what promised to be the hottest day of the season. Pretty soon, some of them began to find difficulty in managing their telegraph wires; the air seemed charged with electricity; the men took their observations, and worked harder than ever. At length the sergeant in charge of one of the largest and busiest stations glanced up quickly from a bunch of dispatches he had just read, examined the barometer with a great deal of care, made a few notes in a huge memorandum book, and scratched off a message, which was handed at once to the telegraph operator sitting a few feet away. In five minutes the government weather officials throughout New England knew that a dangerous storm-centre was rapidly moving toward them; and up went their signals accordingly.

"The Brookville farmers had heard nothing of all this, but they looked at the sky knowingly, and hurried a little at their work. At the quiet old Coburn house the 'women folks' were upstairs asleep, in the lull between dinner and supper; the men were afield, working with all their might.

"'I dunno,' said Patsy, 'but I'll take a bit av a walk wid Shock. Sure, they won't mind ef I'm back before tay.'

"Patsy Dolan and his four-year-old sister Shock (probably so-called in reference to the usual state of her hair) were Boston children, who had been sent into the country for a week by the Missionary Society. Patsy himself was only nine, and knew nothing of the world outside of his native city. As he stepped out of the back door of the old house, leading his little sister, he instinctively glanced over his shoulder. Then he laughed a little at himself.

"'No p'leecemen here!' he said aloud, with a chuckle. 'A feller can kape onto the grass all he wants.'

"It was very slow walking, for Shock was not an accomplished pedestrian, even on brick sidewalks; and here the ground was very uneven.

Besides, it must be confessed that her temper was rather uncertain, and on this particular hot afternoon she constantly required soothing. But Patsy cared little for this. He had been used to taking care of his baby sister almost ever since she was born, and he patiently submitted to her whims, now stopping to disentangle her little bare feet from briery vines, now lifting her in his arms and bearing her over an unusually rough spot. So they went on, across the field, over a tiny brook, through a narrow belt of woods, and out upon an open pasture, which bulged up here and there like a great quilt, with patches of moss and grass, and with round juniper bushes for buttons. At least, this was the image that vaguely suggested itself to Patsy as he tugged his hot little burden along farther and farther away from home.

"Suddenly he stopped and looked up.

"'Sure, it's comin' on night,' said he. 'The sun's gone entirely, it is. We must be goin' back.'

"But Shock had reached the limit of feminine endurance, and declined, with all the firmness of her nature, this unexpected move. She objected to that extent that she sat down hard on the ground, and wailed with heat and weariness.

"Patsy was a little nonplussed, for it was growing very dark. He was acquainted with Shock's resources of resistance, and hesitated to call them forth. While he deliberated he winked and winced at the same moment; a broad drop of water had struck full upon his upturned face.

"'Come out o' that, Shockie,' he cried, 'we *must* go now. The rain is a-comin'!'

"Thereupon Shock made her next move, which was to lie flat on her back and cry louder. She hadn't begun to kick yet, but Patsy knew she would.

"Another great drop fell, and another. It grew bright about them, then suddenly darker than ever, as if somebody had lighted the gas and blown it out.

"Hark! Rumble, rumble, boom, bo-o-m — bo-o-m! Patsy pricked up his ears; for even a city boy knows thunder, though it is half drowned by the roar of the wagons and pavements. Without more words he dived at Shock, and bore her away struggling, across the pasture. It had grown so dark that he could not well see where to put his feet, so he fell once or twice, bruising his wrists badly. But he managed to tumble in a way to save Shock, so it didn't matter.

"There was a moaning and rustling sound in the far-off forests that notched the horizon on every side. Then the wind and the rain joined hands, and rushed forward wildly with a mighty roar that appalled the boy, staggering under his heavy load.

"He halted, and crouched in a little hollow. The voice of the storm now quite swept away the feeble crying of the exhausted child in his arms. As he cast a wild look about him, like a hunted rabbit, a brilliant flash of lightning showed for an instant what promised a refuge which, slight though it might be, seemed blessed compared with this bare field where the storm was searching for him with its terrible, gleaming eyes and hollow voice. If he could only reach that spot, Patsy thought, he would feel easy. It was a single huge elm-tree, like those on the Common, only standing quite alone in the pasture. It would be such a nice place in a thunder-storm — poor Patsy!

"A dim recollection of the prayers the mission people had taught him, came into his mind. But he couldn't think of anything but, 'Now I lay me,' so he concluded to try for the tree first, and say his prayers after he got there.

"He lifted Shock once more in his aching arms, and started.

"But God heard his little heart-prayer above all the booming of the thunder; and this was how He answered it.

"The boy was getting on bravely, when Shock, whose fright was renewed by the motion, gave a sudden struggle. His foot slipped,—down, down he went, into a gully that had lain, unseen, across his path. The bushes broke his fall, but he lay a moment quite breathless and discouraged. But it would not do to remain so; for there was Shock, by no means injured, and crying lustily. Patsy picked himself up, and felt about him until his hand struck the side of a large rock. There was a dry place under one side, which projected slightly. He reached for Shock, and deposited her in this sheltered spot, on some leaves the wind had blown in there last autumn. He wished he could get in, too; but there was barely room for one.

"'Told, told,' moaned Shock, shivering, and drawing up her little limbs.

"Without an instant's hesitation Patsy threw off

his wet jacket, and tucked it round her. In three minutes he knew by her stillness and regular breathing that she was asleep.

"Then he began to be cold — very cold himself. Every whizzing rain-drop seemed like ice, striking on his bare feet and bruised hands. If he could only have that jacket, or put his feet in with Shock under it just for a minute!

"'I don't s'pose she'd know,' he said to himself, with chattering teeth. 'But I won't — no, I won't. A feller must look out fer his sister.'

"Then he remembered the prayers again; and the best thing he could think of was the psalm he had been taught only the Sunday before. He cuddled up as close to the rock as he could, and began:

"'The Lord is my shepherd — I shall — I shall —' Here he forgot, and had to commence again.

"'The Lord is my shepherd, I shall — not — want nothin'. He maketh me to lie down in green pastures —' Patsy paused, and peered into the darkness doubtfully. 'I dunno,' he said, 'as I want —'

"He never finished that sentence. And this was what interrupted him. A great shimmering, glittering flash, that filled all the air, and at the very same moment an awful crash — and the storm beat down upon a little white face, upturned silently to the black sky.

. . . .

"Hallo — hallo — o — o!" The shout rang out clear and strong on the evening air. Far off among the hills the last rumble of thunder was dying away.

"'They must have gone along here,' cried Farmer Coburn; 'hold your lantern, Tom — see, there's their tracks.'

"'Hallo! hallo — o — o! — Why, what —'
What makes Farmer Coburn stop so suddenly, and then dart forward with one of the lanterns? A wee sound, and a sad, sad sight. The sound is the waking voice of Shock, who turns uneasily on her bed of dry leaves; the sight is a little white face, upturned to the star-dotted sky.

"How those rough men bent over the little fellow, the tears running over their cheeks, as they noticed the jacket!

"'He's alive!' shouts Tom, with a half-sob, catching the boy up in his arms, 'he's only stunned,

The lightnin' must have struck round here somewhere, just near enough to knock him over. He's comin' to now!'

"And Patsy comes. As soon as he can talk, he tells them about it.

"'Why,' he says, straightening up in Tom's arms (Shock is sound asleep again, with her tousled head bobbing on Farmer Coburn's shoulder at every step) — 'why, there's the tree, sure —'

"The men looked, and turned away with a shudder. The noble elm would never again lift its green boughs toward the sky. Scorching, rending, shattering, the red lightning had torn its way down the huge trunk, throwing the fragments on every side, and leaving the twisted fibres thrust into the air, white and bare, in a way that told of the terrible force that had had the mastery of them.

"Patsy thought it all over very soberly. He remembered his prayer and his psalm.

"'I dunno —' he said."

As uncle Will ceased, his auditors were very still; thinking, perhaps, how they too had been kept safely from the fury of the tempest on the lonely mountain side.

Ruel now looked out and announced that the storm was over; and indeed there was hardly need of telling it, for the sunbeams came dancing down to the little birch camp with the same story. Out poured the young folks, the girls holding their skirts daintily from contact with the dripping undergrowth, of which, fortunately, there was not an abundance. The brook was much higher than before, and laughed and spoke in deeper tones; as if, like many a young human life, it had grown old during the storm, and was no longer a child.

The whole party now "broke camp" and turned their faces homeward. Their feet they could not keep dry, of course; but they were not far from The Pines, and they knew that aunt Puss was waiting for them with dry socks and a good supper.

Down the path they ran, filling the air with their shouts and laughter. Ruel came last, with a huge bundle of bark, made from the sheets they had used on the hut.

"No use to leave it there," he said, in answer to Randolph's laughing question. "In a week 'twould jest be good fer spiders to live in — all curled up in the sun. Daown 't the house we c'n use it fer your uncle's fires, this tew months."

CHAPTER XI.

THE GREAT BASE BALL MATCH.

THERE was great excitement at The Pines. Randolph and Tom had practised several times with the Readville Base Ball Nine, as I have said, Randolph taking the lead, finally, of the whole club. On a certain afternoon, about a week after the mountain tramp, a dozen or more boys were gathered on the little open plot of ground which the Readville people called the "Common," eagerly discussing a subject which was interesting enough to make their eyes sparkle and their voices all chime in together as they talked.

"Now, hold on, fellows," exclaimed one of the tallest, raising his hand for silence. "We may as well do this business up squarely on the spot. I'll read the challenge, if you'll all keep still."

The boys threw themselves on the ground, and in various easy attitudes prepared to listen.

Randolph, who was speaker, remained standing,

and drawing a paper from his pocket, read as follows :

"The Jamestown High School Nine hereby challenge the Readville Nine to a game of base-ball, to be played on Readville Common, on the afternoon of next Saturday, at three o'clock —"

"Next Saturday!" interjected one of the listeners.

"— five innings to count a game if stopped by rain. League rules to be followed.

"HIRAM BLACK,
"Captain Jamestown B. B. Nine."

A chorus of cheers and cat-calls broke out immediately on the conclusion of the challenge; but Randolph raised his hand once more.

"The question is, Shall we accept? Those in favor say 'Aye!'"

A tremendous shout rent the air.

"Those opposed, 'No!'"

Dead silence.

"It is a vote. Now for positions and players."

So far, there had been no dispute as to Randolph's authority. He had such a pleasant way of getting on with the boys that they followed his lead willingly.

When they came to the choice of positions,

however, there was a little more feeling. As to first, second and third base, the matter was easy enough. There were two fellows who played short-stop well, but they were warm friends, and each was ready to yield to the other.

Dick Manning was acknowledged to be the best pitcher in town, having a "drop twist" which he had gained by days of practice, at odd moments, behind his father's barn, and upon which he greatly prided himself in a modest way.

Up to this point all went smoothly.

"Now, as to catcher," said Randolph. "I know it's a show place, and I don't want to put myself forward. But it's an important game, and I *think* I understand Dick's delivery better than the rest of you. Bert Farnum is a tip-top hand behind the bat, I know; but — "

Randolph hesitated as he saw Bert look down and dig his heel into the ground, half sullenly.

Bert was a graceful player, a strong hitter and swift thrower. His chief trouble was uncertainty. You couldn't depend either on his temper or his nerve in a closely-contested game. Randolph knew this, and now endeavored to smooth over matters by suggesting that Bert should play centre-field at first, and come in for a change during the close of the game, if necessary.

Right and left-fielders were easily appointed, and the boys seized their bats and balls for a couple of hours' practice.

Bert excused himself gruffly, and wandered down by the river alone. He wanted catcher's position for that game, and felt defrauded by his captain.

All the girls from the institute would be sure to come and cluster around the in-field, while the centre-fielder would be stationed away off by himself, with, perhaps, not a single chance to win applause.

Bert's father was one of the wealthiest men in town, and the boy was used to having his own way.

Only yesterday, a fine new catcher's mask had come up from the city. Of course, he had meant to lend it freely to the nine in all their games; but now he resolved he would say nothing about it. The old mask was nearly worn out, and, if struck at certain points, was sure to hurt the wearer.

If Randolph Percival was so particular about catching, he could wear the old thing, for all Bert cared.

Having gone so far as this, the unhappy boy suddenly hit upon another scheme to obtain his revenge. He stopped short and scowled darkly.

"I'll do it," he said to himself; then turned and walked homeward, meditating all the way on the surest means to accomplish his purpose.

It was no less than to bring about the defeat of his own companions. How he succeeded will be seen.

There were only four days before the afternoon set for the match, and uncle Will found his young folks so full of the coming game that they could think of nothing else. Tom, who made a lively third base, seemed for the time to have forgotten his troubles, and entered heartily into the sport. Dick Manning came over from the village every afternoon, and tried his favorite "delivery" with Randolph, who practised catching whenever he could get anybody to throw balls at him. He was continually enticing little Bridget out to perform this duty, which she did with such earnestness and energy that he had to fairly beg for mercy.

It was wonderful to see how the little North Street waif expanded and grew, mentally, physically and morally, in this pure air, and under the

KITTIE AT WORK.

gentle teaching of aunt Puss, who had received her with open arms. The girl's sallow cheeks grew plump and wholesome to look at; her dull eyes brightened; she worked, or tried to, all day, and slept soundly all night. She even learned to play a little, which was the hardest of all. When Randolph had gravely suggested that she could make herself useful by throwing a ball at him, out in the orchard, she accepted the proposition in perfect good faith.

"Sure I wull," said Bridget, taking the ball from Randolph's hand.

Her throws, he found, were just wild enough to give him practice; while their velocity left nothing to be desired. She flung the ball at him as if she were determined to annihilate him on the spot. It was only when he rolled over in the grass, laughing and crying for mercy, that a bewildered smile came into her face.

"Sure ye tould me fire hard, thin," she said slowly, tossing back her long hair.

"So I did, Bridget. And if ever I get back to Boston, I'll propose your name as champion pitcher in the League team!"

The little Irish girl having retired, Pet, who just

then came up, offered to take her place; but her services were gratefully declined. Pet's soft but erratic tosses were already only too familiar to the boys.

Well, the great day came at last. The wagon was filled, immediately after dinner, and the whole party, with uncle Will at the reins, drove over to Readville. They stationed themselves on the edge of the base ball grounds, where Randolph said they could obtain a good view, and their team would not be in the way of the players. The air was warm, but a gentle westerly breeze, mountain-cooled, prevented discomfort from the heat.

By two o'clock, groups of young people, in twos and threes, began to stroll toward the Common.

Already a number of players were on hand engaged in vigorous practice, their jaunty uniforms showing prettily against the green, closely-cropped ball-field. The Jamestown nine wore blue stockings and gray suits; the "Readvilles," white, with red stockings.

The crowd increased. At about a quarter before three, two of the players, one from each nine, separated at a distance from the Common, and came to it from different directions.

One of them was the captain of the "Jamestowns," a rough, black-eyed fellow, whom nobody liked, but who was a fine player. The other was Bert Farnum.

As the hour for the game drew near, the excitement in the Percival wagon was at fever heat. Tom and his cousins were in the field, practising, and the girls watched eagerly every play the two made Randolph wore the old mask, and worked steadily with Dick, a little to one side. Quite a crowd of Jamestown people had come over to witness the game and cheer for their nine, who were considerably heavier than their opponents. The knowing ones among the spectators gave their opinion that if the "Readvilles" were to win, they would have to do it by spryness in the field; the "Jamestowns" would bat more effectively, and throw well. Bert Farnum was spoken of as a splendid thrower, on whom much depended.

"They say that Boston fellow, Percival, is a master hand," said one broad-shouldered young farmer who had sauntered up within hearing of the wagon-party "Jest look at him now, practisin'! He ketches them swift, twisty balls like clockwork!"

Kitty and Bess pinched each other, and their faces glowed with pride.

"I knew it," whispered Kittie confidentially to Pet, "but I like to hear somebody else say it, just the same."

Further conversation was suddenly hushed by a movement among the players. Three o'clock had arrived, and in presence of the umpire the two captains tossed up a cent. The "Readvilles" won the toss, and sent their opponents to the bat.

As the red-stockings walked past them into the field, the Jamestown captain winked at Bert, who nodded slightly in return, blushing at the same time and glancing over his shoulder to see if he was observed.

"Low ball — play!" called the umpire.

Dick Manning drew himself up, looking carelessly about the field; then suddenly, with a swift movement, sent the white ball whizzing directly over the plate, about two feet from the ground.

"One strike!" shouted the umpire.

The Jamestowner looked surprised, and before he had gathered himself for the next ball it was past him again and in the hands of Randolph, who waited till the umpire called "Strike, two!" and then ran up behind the bat, adjusting the old mask over his face.

The next two balls delivered were wide. The third was just right, and the Jamestowner hit with all his force. It soared far up in the air, toward the centre-field.

"Bert! Bert Farnum!" cried Randolph as two or three of the fielders started for the ball.

Bert ran, and stretched out his hands — a little awkwardly, his friends thought. The next moment the ball struck the ground six feet away, and the striker was safe on second base.

A prolonged "Oh-h-h!" came involuntarily from the crowd, and Bert returned with a sullen air to his station, after fielding the ball.

The Jamestowns now succeeded in getting the striker and another man round the bases. Randolph put out the third, by running a long distance under a foul fly, almost reaching the wagon before he secured it.

The "Readvilles" were retired without making a run. Score, 2 to 0, in favor of Jamestown. The girls clenched their hands in silence, while the Jamestown people on the other side of the grounds cheered lustily.

The game proceeded, and was contested hotly at every point. The visitors seemed possessed with but one ambition, and that was to knock the ball down to centre. Time and again it started in that direction, but dropped short, or into the hands of one of the other fielders.

At last the ninth inning was reached. The score was a tie — eight to eight. "Jamestown" came to the bat, and two men went out in quick succession, one on a foul fly, the other at first base. The third striker got the ball just where he wanted it, and sent it high up in Bert's direction.

Now, Bert had already begun to repent of the treacherous part he was playing. Here was a chance to redeem himself. He made a desperate run backward for the ball, but tripped and fell just as it was coming to his hands. Again he heard that long note of dismay from his friends. The sound nerved him. Leaping to his feet, he darted after the ball like a deer, and, picking it up lightly, as it rolled, faced about. The runner was making the round of the bases, amid the shouts and jeers of the Jamestown people who had come over to see the game.

Bert gathered himself for a mighty effort, and,

drawing back his arm, threw the ball with all his strength. Randolph was waiting for it eagerly, with his foot on the home-plate. It seemed impossible that the ball could get there in time, and the Jamestowners cheered more lustily than ever, as the blue stockings went flying along the base-line toward home; but still more swiftly came the ball, sent with unerring aim from Bert's far-away arm.

Just a wee fraction of a second before the runner touched the plate the ball settled into Randolph's hands, which swung round like lightning, and Jamestown was out — score, 8 to 8.

On coming in with his side for their last turn at the bat, Bert found himself all at once a hero.

"Never was such a throw seen on the grounds!" they said; and poor Bert hung his head, and answered not a word.

The spectators were now fairly breathless with excitement. The score tied, and Readville at the bat for the last time.

Tom, whose turn it was, took his place amid encouraging shouts from his side. After a nervous "strike," he made a good hit that carried him to second, where he seemed likely to be left, as the next two at the bat struck easy flies, and went out.

It was Bert's turn. Heretofore he had purposely struck out every time he came to the bat. Now his hands clenched the stick firmly, and he braced his feet as if he meant business. The crowd saw the slight movement, and cheered to encourage him.

"Strike one!" called the umpire, as the ball flew over the plate a little higher than Bert wanted it.

"Strike two!"

Still not just right. Bert waited calmly. The crowd were silent, and looked downcast. Suddenly they gave a wild cheer. Hats were flung into the air, and handkerchiefs waved. Bert had made a terrific hit, sending the ball far beyond the right-fielder. In another moment Tom had reached home, and scored the winning run — score, Readvilles, 9; Jamestowns, 8.

The great match was finished.

CHAPTER XII.

HUNTED TO EARTH.

AS soon as the excitement over the base-ball match had died away, Tom's moodiness returned. It was now near the end of August, and the little party at the Pines began to show signs of breaking up. Kittie and her sister, with Tom, were to meet their father and mother at Portland on the twenty-fifth of the month, returning to Boston in season for school. Randolph, too, was due in the Latin School ranks on September fifth; Pet received a letter from her family, telling her to join them at the mountains at about the same time.

As the remaining days of vacation rapidly dwindled, the fun, on the contrary, increased. Bert Farnum had a long talk with Randolph, shortly after the match, and made a clean breast of his treachery, telling him how he had suffered from remorse at the unmanly part he had played in the earlier part of the great game, and how repentant he was for the whole affair. The result of this confession was that the two boys became firm friends, and Bert, in company with Dick Manning and a good-natured sister Polly, often joined the Bostonians in their mountain tramps, hay-cart rides, and other good times.

Old Sebattis and his wife were reported as encamped near the county road, fifteen miles away. Of course, nothing had been heard of the watch, the secret of its whereabouts being locked in the breast of one unhappy boy.

One hot, sultry afternoon, when the rest had gone off to the woods on a picnic, Tom started alone for his favorite hiding-place in the cliff near the alder run. He walked slowly down the path, looking neither to right nor left, and seeing nothing of the beauty of flower and bird and tree about him. He was saying over and over to himself, "I'll do it! I won't stand it any longer! I'll do it this very afternoon!"

He made his way across the field, down through the pasture, and along the dry brook-channel to the drooping beech-tree. Glancing about him carelessly, from mere habit, he swung himself up to the trunk and clambered into the snug nook among the ferns.

Had he, for once, scrutinized his surroundings more earnestly, and peered around the corner of the large fallen bowlder at the foot of the cliff, he might have seen two dark eyes fastened upon him, from among the undergrowth. Their gaze was so full of spite and low cunning that it would have been well for Tom had he caught a glimpse of them and sprung away at once. But without a thought of danger, his mind concentrated on one object alone, he reached his high perch, and seated himself on a rock to regain his breath.

Already his face had a better expression than it had worn for weeks. His lips were set, as if with a firm and noble resolve ; his eyes flashed with the light that always shines full on the face that is turned toward the Right. It was plain that Tom had made up his mind at last, and was happier for it, whatever might be the consequences.

After resting a few moments, he carefully removed a few odd bits of stone and moss from the mouth of a crevice in the rock, and drew out Pet's watch. He at once examined it thoroughly, holding it to his ear as he had done on a previous occasion.

"Yes," said he to himself, with great satisfaction, "it's all right. One good rub, to brighten it up, and in fifteen minutes it shall be in uncle Will's hands."

He drew a piece of flannel from his pocket, and polished the case of the pretty little timepiece, inside and out, until it shone so that he could see his own face reflected in the gold. Then he placed it carefully in an inner pocket, and rising to his feet with a sigh of relief, stepped down toward the slanting trunk of the beech, on which he was prepared to descend, as usual.

He had no sooner stooped for this purpose, however, when he started back with an involuntary cry of alarm.

About six feet below him, staring upward with a face full of malignant cunning, was Sebattis Megone, in the very act of seizing the swaying limbs of the tree to mount the ledge. The moment he saw that he was detected, he released his grasp on the boughs, and stood still, looking up at Tom with an ugly grin.

"Ugh!" he grunted, Indian-fashion. "What boy do on rocks? What he want in woods?"

Tom glanced about him hastily. If the man had

evil intentions, there was no way of escape. It seemed as if he could feel the little watch beating against his own heart. He tried to answer with an appearance of carelessness.

"I come here most every day and read," he said. "It's cool in the woods."

"What climb up high for?"

"There's a good place here to sit down. I like to be alone, sometimes, don't you, Sebattis?"

The good-will of the tone was lost on the Indian, who evidently knew more than he cared to tell.

"Where Gold-hair's watch?" he asked suddenly and fiercely, to throw Tom off his guard.

"It was lost that day she fell into the lake."

"Yis. Me remember. See!" and Sebattis scowled darkly as he laid his hand on a scar where the broken window, probably, had cut his forehead.

"I am sorry you were hurt," began Tom, nervously.

"You know where watch is. Give me!"

"Why do you think I know about it?" Tom wanted to gain time. His only hope was that some one might stray down into the woods within reach of his voice. As to the cliff, he knew well enough, for he had often examined it, and even tried the feat in fun once or twice, that it could not be scaled. From the hollow where he stood, the face of the rock slanted outward above him, rendering escape in that direction out of the question.

"If you no give me, I come up and take watch — maybe hurt you!" snarled the Indian in his guttural tones.

"Hold on," said poor Tom, at his wit's end; more anxious, now, for the safety of the watch than for himself. "It will be easier for me to come down than for you to climb way up here."

"You come then — quick!"

The man was plainly growing angry, and laid his hand on his knife as he spoke, by way of menace.

But Tom had no idea of coming down. Instead of that, he suddenly drew back a step, and shouted at the top of his lungs,

"*Help! Help! Tim, uncle Percival! Help!*"

For a moment the Indian seemed taken aback at this unlooked-for move, glancing fearfully over his shoulder as if he expected to hear Tim's sturdy footfalls. Then his rage got the better of him, and, grasping the branches once more, he began to clamber upward.

Fortunately, being rather stout, he could not manage the ascent quite so nimbly as Tom. The boy, pale as death, sprang back into the furthest corner of the cavity, intending to fight to the last, in defence of the watch, the loss of which had brought such sorrow to Pet, and such disgrace and unhappiness to his own summer vacation at his uncle's.

What would have been the result of such a struggle, I cannot tell. The Indian was armed, and the boy would have been but a baby in his hands, if the issue depended upon mere strength. But at this moment a strange thing happened.

When Tom drew back into the hollow formed by the angle of the rocks, he crowded in among the ferns and thick moss further than he had ever been before. As he did so, he threw one despairing look about him for a weapon. What seemed to be a loose stone caught his eye. It was covered with many years' growth of lichens, but it came up easily in his hand. As he was stooping to raise it, what was his astonishment to find beneath it a dark opening into what appeared a sort of inner cave, the mouth of which had been concealed by rubbish.

With the instinct of a hunted animal, as he had

the boughs of the beech-tree creak under the weight of his enemy, he tore aside the rocks and moss which were easily dislodged and in a moment more he was in the hole, pulling the largest stone within reach over the mouth of his strange retreat as he disappeared within it.

His first sensation was one of relief. The Indian, he knew, would hesitate about entering a trap like this, where his unseen foe might spring upon him from any side. Already his footsteps were heard, on the stones above, and his short, surprised grunt when he found his victim had sunk into the ground like a mole. He was beginning to cautiously remove the rubbish from the opening, when Tom thought it was time to beat a further retreat.

At first, plunging suddenly into darkness out of the sunny afternoon, he had been able to see nothing. Now the few rays of light that entered enabled him to distinguish the nature of his surroundings. He found that he was in a little rocky chamber, perhaps ten feet square and half as many high, partly natural and partly cleared by the hand of man; as he could tell by the regular arrangement of stones here and there. At the further end was a blacker space than anywhere else. He moved across the cave, and found that this was the entrance to an inner tunnel or passage-way, apparently leading to still further recesses. The Indian had now ceased work, and Tom felt more nervous than when he could hear him scratching and digging at the mouth of the cave. There seemed nothing for it but to keep on, in the black passage, where the darkness, at least, would favor him. He had to get down on his hands and knees, as this inner opening was less than three feet in diameter; and in this way he crawled ahead, into the depths of the little cave.

Up to this moment he had never stopped to reason out the possible cause for such a queer, underground chamber. Now it suddenly flashed upon him that it must be the secret passage-way that his uncle had told about; for although Tom had not been in the room when Mr. Percival had described this ancient provision for escape in case of sudden attack, he had heard his sisters speak of it afterward. Where it came out, he did not know; but the thought that he must be moving toward the house gave him new courage.

Making as little noise as possible, he crept along the passage-way, hoping every minute that it would expand to a size sufficient to allow of his walking erect. After a short halt for rest, he started on again, having made such good progress that he believed he must be half way to the house. Two or three times he bumped his head, but he paid little attention to bruises. So far he was safe, with the watch in his pocket, from his ugly pursuer.

He had not gone a dozen feet, however, when he came to a second halt, his heart beating fast. What was the matter with the boy? With a good chance of escape before him, and half of the tunnel passed, he ought to have been pressing forward. But here he was, crouching almost flat to the earth, stock still, as if afraid to advance another inch. What could be the matter? Tom could have told you very quickly, what he had been suspecting for the last five minutes, and what was now true beyond a question. *The passage-way was contracting!* Instead of growing wider and higher it was now so small that he could barely squeeze through on his hands and knees. Presently he lay down at full length, and wriggled along, the perspiration pouring from every inch of his body, the earth falling in a fine shower about his hair and neck. What if the tunnel should come to an end? Should he remain there wedged in this terrible place, *buried alive?* Ah, this was not all that made Tom tremble, and urge his way still more earnestly through the narrowing tunnel. When he had paused, a moment before, he had heard, plainly as through a speaking-tube, a slight disturbance, a sound of scratching, the fall of a distant rock in the passage behind him. He could not hide from himself the meaning of those sounds. The Indian had explored the cave, had discovered his method of escape, and was now actually in the tunnel, in close pursuit,

CHAPTER XIII.

FOUND AT LAST.

MR. PERCIVAL had spent a busy half-day in the open air, superintending matters on his farm. There were early potatoes to be dug, heavily laden branches of apple and pear trees to be propped up, and a small, low-lying piece of meadow-land to be mown. Slowly the deliberate oxen had plodded to and fro, with the heavy cart creaking and thumping behind them; while Tim or Ruel tramped beside, urging them on with an occasional " Haw! Ha' Bright! Gee! Star!"

Mr. Percival was a good farmer, and nothing " shiftless " could be found on his place. The barn was always fresh and sweet, fences and walls upright; and even the pigs seemed to enjoy a clean, dry corner in their pen where they could lie in the sunshine and grunt contentedly in their sleep.

In the afternoon the men had their work well laid out, and the master retired for an hour or two, as was often his custom, to the "Den." The little windows, above and on the side, were wide open, the air that floated in was cooled by the shadows of the many-elled old house. Now and then came the faint sounds of Tim's encouraging shout to his oxen, a cackle or long-drawn crow from the poultry-yard, the bark of a dog, digging at a squirrel-hole under the wall.

Mr. Percival stretched himself out comfortably in an old cane-seat chair, having taken from its shelf a copy of Thackeray's "Henry Esmond," and began to read. As the story was perfectly familiar to him, he opened the book in the middle, striking into the narrative where Colonel Esmond — one of the finest gentlemen in story — went to the wars under gallant old General Webb.

The air was soft and warm, and the out-door rustle of wind and bough so soothing, after the hard forenoon's work, that Mr. Percival's fancy began to play him queer tricks. He thought that lovely Beatrix Esmond was nodding and smiling to him through the little casement, and he was about to speak to her when he returned to consciousness with a start, laughed to himself as he saw the bit of apple-bough, with sunlight playing on the leaves, that had tricked him; fixed his eyes on the book again, read six lines, and went sound asleep.

His dreams still followed the course of the book he had been reading. He thought he was in England, and that Ruel was the exiled heir to the throne, whom it was his business to support; but that aunt Puss persisted in wearing diamonds at court and purring constantly (the maltese kittens had trotted into the Den and one of them jumped into Mr. Percival's lap) while Ruel himself proceeded to ride about the room on a base-ball bat, in a manner quite inconsistent with royal dignity. Beatrix then came on the scene, but she talked with a brogue and confided to him, Mr. Percival, that her real name was Bridget, and that she had a yoke of oxen which were trained to gallop off with a fire-engine at every alarm. In fact, the oxen (who had been all the time eating hay behind Ruel's throne) now advanced, and holding a hose-pipe in their paws — they were now very large red cats, he noticed carelessly — began to play on the fire.

The curious part of it was that the hose-pipe did not play water at all, but cannon-balls. Indeed, it was not hose, on closer view, but cannon, which aunt Puss, commanding the English forces, was firing against the French.

Boom! Boom! went the cannon. The noise of the conflict was terrible. Aunt Puss stopped purring and rode off on one of the cats, which were now oxen once more.

Boom! Boom! Boom! It fairly shook the room — no, the fort — that is — yes — what! — could it be? Mr. Percival rubbed his eyes and sat upright in his chair. Thackeray had dropped upon the floor; a few gray hairs in his lap, and a fading sensation of warmth in the same locality, betrayed the recent presence of Kittie. But —

Boom! boom! boom! The cannonading went on! Now fairly awake, Mr. Percival recognized the fact that there was an energetic pounding against the floor directly beneath his feet.

"Bless me!" exclaimed the good man aloud, jumping up and surveying the carpet suspiciously, "what can it be?"

The cellar, he knew, extended under the Den. That is, the base of the old chimney had been there, and — ah! that long disused passage! The little stone chamber under the arches, where one could stifle so easily, the girls had thought! A muffled cry, sounding strangely like "Help!" now accompanied the blows, which seemed lessening in force.

Hesitating no longer, and dismissing from his mind the silly ghost-stories that had been handed down in the family, from old times, he knelt and tore up the strip of straw matting that covered the spot at which the blows seemed to be directed; at the same time knocking back, in answer.

"It may be some of the boys' fun," he said to himself, "but it won't do to run any risks."

The straw matting being removed, there appeared a square, dimly marked out in the flooring, by the edges of boards which had apparently been let in, long after the neighboring portions.

"The old trap-door!"

Mr. Percival recognized the place instantly; at the same time he was puzzled to know how to act. For the door had long ago been removed, and these short sections of planks nailed down in its place.

"Hold on!" he shouted. "I'll be back in a minute!"

Very nimbly, for a man of his years, he hurried out of the room, and presently returned with tools — an axe, a large, heavy chisel, a saw, and a kind of sharp-pointed hammer, like an ice-pick. With the aid of these, he soon had the end of one board, then another, pried up. It must be confessed that he was startled by the apparition that emerged from the opening thus effected. Could that be Tom! A face, deadly white, but streaked with perspiration and dust, and bleeding from a bruise on the forehead; clothes, hands, every part of him, covered with dirt; eyes half-blinded by the sudden light, form trembling from head to foot; it was altogether a strange figure to come up through uncle Will's floor — but Tom it was, beyond a doubt.

"O uncle Will," he sobbed brokenly, the tears running over his mud-stained cheeks, "I'm so sorry. Here's the watch!"

And to Mr. Percival's utter bewilderment, the boy laid Pet's little watch in his hands, safe and whole.

It was a long story, but Tom managed to tell it. At the very first, he spoke with a shudder of the Indian, and Mr. Percival despatched Ruel and Tim to the woods, rightly judging that the pursuit of Tom had ceased. The men returned within a few minutes and reported that Sebattis had been seen limping away toward the road, covered with mud. He had turned and shaken his fist at them, but on the whole seemed more frightened than angry, and mainly anxious to get as far away from the farm as possible.

"And now about the watch," said Mr. Percival gravely, but kindly, as soon as the farm-hands had left the room.

Tom hung his head still lower, but launched manfully into his confession.

"I took it out of Pet's pocket for fun," he said, "very soon after we started on our walk, that morning. Then I tucked it into Kitty's sacque, with the chain hanging out."

"Where Moll saw it!" exclaimed Mr. Percival, a light breaking in on him.

"Yes, sir, I suppose so. After that, we came to the Indians, and Pet fell into the pond, and I forgot all about it. Just as I was going to bed, I heard the girls say something about a watch being lost, and it came to me that it was my fault. I felt awfully about it that night, and hardly slept a bit. Next morning I tried to get a chance to tell you about it — do you remember, sir? but you were busy; and instead of *making* you hear, or owning up at once, about my carelessness and foolish trick, I thought I would put it off; perhaps the watch would be found; perhaps the Indians took it, after all."

"But why didn't you tell me frankly, that afternoon, my boy?"

"I was ashamed to; and after the trial, it was all the harder. Then — I found the watch! It was tucked into an old stump, near the spot where the Indian babies, the little pappooses, had been playing. I suppose one of them had picked it up and hidden it there.

"Now was the time, I know, sir, when I ought to have told. But every minute made it harder. I was afraid Randolph would be ashamed of me, and the girls wouldn't like me, and you would be angry for all the trouble I had made, and the expense of the sheriffs and everything. Besides," continued the boy eagerly, "really and truly, sir, I did mean, every day, to give the watch back — every day. But — somehow — it grew harder and harder, and I didn't. It began to seem now as if I had stolen it!"

It was a poor, miserable story of a weak boy's

foolishness; for Tom was weak, and cowardly, too. A little manliness at the start would have prevented all the shame and wretchedness.

Don't you see how he could do it? Do you wonder how he could wish to keep the secret, for such silly reasons?

Stop a moment. Are you quite sure that you yourself would have done differently? Have you not, even now, some little uncomfortable secret hidden in your heart, that you had rather father or mother would not know? If you have, let me beg you to turn down a leaf, or put in a book-mark, at this very page, and go this moment to those dear hearts who are so ready to hear everything and forgive everything with that wonderful love of theirs which is most of anything on earth, like the love of our Father above.

Tom kept nothing back, but related all his faults, his concealments, his misgivings. At length his narrative reached the point at which we stopped in the last chapter, where he felt the passage narrowing, and the Indian following behind.

"I made one more push," he said, "and this time wasn't I glad to find that the tunnel was just a little larger? It was like an hour-glass; and I had passed the narrowest part, in the middle! As soon as I was sure of this, I felt about for some means to block the passage of the Indian. I dug with all my might into the earth, and pretty soon struck a good-sized rock. This almost filled the space, and, with the loose dirt around it, I hoped would discourage Sebattis — as I guess it did.

"I struck my forehead on a sharp stone and made it bleed, though I didn't know that till just now. At the end of the tunnel was a little stone chamber and a half a dozen wooden steps leading up to the floor. These were so old that they crumbled when I stepped on them; but I managed to climb up on the side wall, and strike with a rock on the boards overhead. I was afraid every moment that the Indian might be upon me, and oh! I was so glad when I heard your voice!"

What further words passed between the repentant boy and his uncle, Tom never told. An hour later he came out of the Den, walked up to Pet (who had returned from her ride) with a white face but firm step, and placing the watch and chain in her hands, said, with trembling lips,

"I took it for fun, Pet, and was ashamed to tell —"

He could get no further, and Pet, after one glance at his face, forgave him on the spot. Nor did she ever ask him a single question about her lost watch.

CHAPTER XIV.

QUIET DAYS AT THE PINES.

WHO can describe the long, peaceful days of early autumn in the country? To our boys and girls at uncle Will's, the hours were full of delight, though there were no more hair-breadth escapes, and no fatiguing expeditions undertaken.

On the day after Tom's adventure with the Indian, Mr. Percival visited the old ledge with his men, and placing a charge of blasting powder in the mouth of the cave, tumbled the overhanging rocks together in such a way that the passage was closed forever. The boy slowly regained his cheerfulness, and, rather shyly, took part in the pleasuring of the rest.

Only two days now remained before the party was to break up.

There was little time for story-telling, for the girls were busy, packing various collections of ferns, moss, and other memorials of their good times in field and forest; and their kind host was occupied from morning till night, in overseeing the fall work on the farm.

One evening, however, as they were sitting under one of the aged elms, near the house, the conversation turned upon mountains and mountain climbing.

"Did you and that boy — wasn't his name Fred? — ever have any more adventures together?" asked Pet.

"Oh, yes, a good many, my dear. If you're not too sleepy, I can tell you about a bit of a dangerous climb I once had myself, when we two were abroad together."

The moonlight rested softly on the little circle, and on uncle Will's face, as he talked. Pet put her hand in his, and begged him to go on. It was their last story for the summer.

"We were both pretty well tired out, one July evening when we reached Chamounix. Fred could bear mountain climbing, and, what was worse, muleback riding, much better than I, so that, while I was glad to find my way to my room, in the top of the queer old hotel, at an early hour in the evening, Fred remained in the parlor, busily studying up

QUIET MOMENTS

maps and guides for an excursion over the Mer de Glace to the 'Garden,' a small, fertile spot, surrounded by eternal ice, in the very heart of the mountains.

"Next morning, he was off at four o'clock, leaving me to spend the day quietly in the valley. I was disturbed but once more before rising; this time by a herd of goats, who scrambled along under my windows, with bells tingling merrily enough.

"In the course of the forenoon, I strolled away, book in hand, following the course of the Arve for a little while, and then striking off at right angles, up the banks of a small brook, which joins the larger stream just above the village.

"The air was soft and sweet with summer sunlight and the breath of the silent forests, reaching from my feet, higher and higher, until the front rank looked on those desolate, glittering fields of snow that crown Mount Blanc.

"Beside the brook the velvety turf was dotted with wild forget-me-nots and pansies, growing there as peacefully as if they were not in the very track of last year's avalanche.

"At length I came to a spot where the brook

had in ages past strewn its own path with fragments of huge rocks, which it had loosened and thrown down from some far-off height, where the foot of man never trod.

"One gigantic bowlder lay completely across the original bed of the stream, and rose like a wall beside the water, that turned out of its way, and ran off with a good-natured laugh.

"The sun here lay warm and bright, just counteracting the chill breeze that came from the glaciers through the narrow gorge. I gathered a few dry sticks, kindled a fire, merely for company, and nestled comfortably down into an easy corner to read the rocks, the brook, the sky, and, if there were time left, my book, which, if I remember rightly, was 'Redgauntlet.'

"How long I sat there I cannot tell. It must have been two or three hours, for it was past noon when I looked at my watch, threw the smouldering firebrands into the brook, and rose to return to the hotel.

"As I did so, I noticed half a dozen foot-steps in the steep, sandy bank that formed the side of the ravine at this point. It suddenly occurred to me that I had read in my guide-book, while I was sitting in my own room, six months before, of a certain waterfall, which, from the description, must surely be on this brook. Yes, I recollected the base of the zig-zag path, that we had seen as we rode along the valley, on our way from Tête Noire, late the preceding afternoon.

"I was feeling much refreshed and rested by my siesta, and, by a short cut up over this embankment, I could doubtless strike that path after a three minutes' scramble, as some one had evidently done before me.

"So I would have a little adventure, and see one of the sights of Chamounix all by myself.

"Certainly there was nothing rash in this resolve, or formidable in the undertaking; though a certain feebleness resulting from a recent ill turn at Geneva should have warned me against tasking my strength too severely.

"At any rate, at it I went, laughing at the easiness of the ascent as I followed the broad footsteps of my predecessor. My calculation was that I should come out on the path at a point about seventy-five to one hundred feet above my starting-place.

"Before I had proceeded far, however, the convenient tracks abruptly ceased. Beyond, and on each side, there was nothing but the gravelly bank, with here and there a big rock ready to drop at the lightest touch.

"Plainly enough, the first climber had become discouraged at this point, and had picked his way to the bottom again. As I looked back I was startled to observe the elevation which I had reached, and I involuntarily crouched closer to the earth, with a sensation as of tipping over backwards.

"The movement, slight as it was, dislodged a clump of stones and sand, which went rolling and and plunging down at a great rate to the brook, the sound of whose waters was now hardly audible. No wonder the man had given it up! Should I go on, or literally back down, as he had done?

"My pluck was stirred, and although I heartily wished Fred was on hand with his sympathetic courage, I resolved to complete what I had begun.

"It was tough work. Hands and knees now — and carefully placed every time, at that. Once I nearly lost my balance by the unexpected yielding of a large stone, which gave way under my foot. How fearfully long it was before I heard it smite on the bowlders below! I knew if I slipped, or missed one step, the impetus of a yard would send me after the stone. As I looked over my shoulder, it seemed like clinging to the slope of a cathedral roof, where a puff of wind might be fatal.

"There was no question now as to the course I must take. It was 'Excelsior' in sober earnest — only I didn't have the inspiration of a maiden, with a tear in her bright blue eye, looking on.

"Steeper and steeper! I was panting heavily in the rarified atmosphere, and trembling from exhaustion. It was so terribly lonely. Nothing but the dark forms of the trees, the waste of ice and snow, and now and then a bird, winging its way silently over the gulf, until my brain whirled as I watched its slow flight.

"By to-morrow they would miss me, and organize a search, with Fred at their head. They would find my footprints beside the brook, where I had leaped carelessly across after pansies; then they would come upon the blackened traces of the little fire, and the loosened gravel of the steep bank; they would look upward with a shudder, and search the harder. Pretty soon one of them would lean over a crevice among the bowlders, shrink back with a cry of horror, and beckon to the others. All this if I failed by one step!

"Still I worked on laboriously, often pausing for giddiness or a want of breath, and digging with my finger-nails little hollows in the hard bank for my feet.

"Once or twice a long, tough root of grass saved me; and soon, to my joy, straggling bushes, strong enough to support a few pounds of weight, thrust their tops through the sand-bed.

"Then came scrubby trees, cedar and fir, oftentimes growing straight out from a vertical face of rock, and quivering from root to tip as I drew myself cautiously up.

"I shall never forget the agony of the moment when one of them came out entirely, and let me fall backward. Fortunately its comrades were near enough to save me, though it was with rough hands.

"To shorten the story, I climbed at last out upon a small, level spot, which proved to be the longed-for path.

"Following it painfully up for a few rods, I reached a little hut, where I found a kind old Frenchwoman, who refreshed me with food and drink, helped me to make my tattered clothes presentable, and held up her hands after the demonstrative fashion of her nation, when she heard of my climb.

"'Had any one ever ascended to the cataract upon that side?'" I asked.

"'*Jamais, monsieur; jamais, jamais!*'" (Never, monsieur; never, never.)

"And could she tell me the height from the valley?"

"*Mille pieds.*"

"A thousand feet! Well, I had had mountain-climbing enough for one day, and after a visit to the Cascade, which was close by, I hobbled down the easy path and back to the hotel, to read 'Redgauntlet,' until bedtime.

"When Fred got back, and heard the story, his eyes were round enough, as he declared he would not leave me behind again, to play invalid, until we came in sight of the wharf in East Boston. And he kept his promise."

CHAPTER XV.

GOOD-BYE!

THE morning of the last day at The Pines was full of sunshine. Ruel's voice was heard, as early as five o'clock, out by the barn. The young folks, by a preconcerted plan, all rose at sunrise, in order to make as long a day as possible, and joined the men, who were milking.

"Well, well," said Ruel, looking up from his foaming pail, into which the white streams were drumming merrily, "you *hev* got up with the birds this time, sartin!"

"We didn't want to lose a minute," answered Kittie rather sadly. "O Ruel, I wish we could stay till winter!"

"'Twouldn't do," replied the other, shaking his head. "Thar's plenty to do in the city, an' everybody has his place. Sometimes I've wished—" but Ruel did not say what he had wished.

"Ruel," said Bess, after a moment's silence,

"why couldn't you come to Boston in the winter and work. Surely you could earn more money there?"

Ruel shook his head again, more soberly than before.

"My place is here with your uncle," he replied. "I was born and brought up in these parts. I'm at home in the woods, an' I couldn't bear to walk raound on bricks an' stones. No, here I be, an' here I must stay."

"But wouldn't you like to spend a month in the city? You said the other day you had never been there."

The old trapper seemed at a loss for words, but presently answered: "I can't jest tell ye haow I feel abaout it, Bess, but somehaow I sh'd feel shet in, and kept away from the blue sky. What with lookin' aout fer teams an' horses an' folks, an' seein' all sorts o' strange sights, an' p'raps thinkin' o' makin' money — why, I'm afeerd I shouldn't feel so much of a man. In the woods it's all so still that I can almost hear the trees a-growin'. Then a bird flies through the baoughs overhead, an' I look up an' see all the firs with their leetle crosses, and the pines pointin' up, an' so I keep lookin' higher, an' thar's the blue, an' the clouds, an' I remember who's up thar, an' who made woods an' birds an' all!"

The little company of daintily dressed boys and girls felt awed into silence as they listened to this outburst from the rough preacher, sitting on a milking-stool, and never forgetting his work, as he talked. It was a sermon they would remember long after the old barn and The Pines and Ruel himself were hundreds of miles away.

"What hev ye planned fer to-day?" said Ruel in his ordinary, quiet tones, breaking the silence that had followed his earnest words.

"O, there's a lot of packing. The 'silver rags' are to be tied up, to take home. And we're going to every spot on the farm where we've had good times this lovely summer!"

"I was thinkin' that p'raps you might like to wind up with a little fishin' trip this afternoon."

"O good! Where shall we go?"

"Right daown by where we were cuttin' wood last winter — remember? — thar's a little brook that always has plenty of trout in it."

"That's first-rate!" exclaimed Randolph. "The girls can take a lunch — just a small one, without much fuss — and Tom and I will furnish a string of trout."

"They're awful little," added Ruel, "but they're sweet's nuts. You can ketch a dozen in fifteen minutes."

The boys had been fishing several times during their vacation, but had never taken the girls along.

The forenoon was full of both duty and play. Trunks were filled to the brim and sat upon; great bundles of birch bark were tied up and labeled. All the cattle received toothsome bits of their favorite varieties of food, and were bidden good-bye, with strokings and pattings, all of which they received with abundance of patience and long sighs.

Meanwhile aunt Puss busied herself in preparing an appetizing little lunch for the last picnic, and for the morrow's journey. All the men were hard at work in the potato patch and the orchard. At about three o'clock Ruel threw down his hoe and informed the boys, with one of his quiet laughs, that Mr. Percival had given him a half-day vacation.

"Get your party together," said he, "and meet me in fifteen minutes out here by the pasture bars.

I'll have the bait ready. You can bring the poles you used last Monday."

With baskets for lunch and for final collections of fresh ferns, the girls joined the rest, and all started down the long pasture lane through which they had watched the cattle wandering slowly homeward so many times during the past weeks. By special invitation the little Irish girl was included in the party, much to her delight.

In a few minutes they were in the shade of the forest. The pines whispered softly to them, and the birches, in the little clearings here and there, fluttered their dainty leaves in the sunlight overhead. No one felt much like talking and almost the only sound was the occasional call of a thrush or the piping of a locust in the tree-tops. At length the brook was reached. The boys rigged their fishing tackle and were soon busily creeping down the banks of the little stream, uttering an exclamation now and then, as they captured or lost a lively trout.

The girls threw themselves down on a mossy bank, close beside a tiny spring which Ruel pointed out. There were fir-trees intermingled with the pines and hemlocks around it ; and on its brink a fringe of ferns bent over the clear water. Randolph had known of the place before, but his cousins had never found it.

When the fishermen came back, they found lunch spread upon napkins, and awaiting only the trout. These Ruel took in hand, dressing and broiling them with the deftness of an old camper. Sheets of birch bark served for plates, and the boys whittled out knives and forks from the twigs of the same tree. Bridget, whose first camping experience it was, sat motionless, in a state of stupefied wonder and delight.

"Now, sir," said Pet, addressing Randolph, "we need one thing more. As it's a farewell meeting, we ought to have a poem, an original poem."

"O, his brother —" exclaimed Kittie.

"No," said Pet decisively, "that won't do. We'll give you just twenty minutes to write one, Randolph. If your brother can do it, of course you can. One, two, three, begin!"

Fortunately for the boy, who was extremely confused by the sudden request and the six bright eyes bent upon him, he had been in the habit of scribbling in a note book such bits of verse as occurred to him when he was by himself; and this very spring had suggested itself as a pretty subject for a poem. When the time was up, accordingly, he came forward with the following, handing it with a low bow to Miss Pet, who read it aloud:

DOLLIE'S SPRING.

Deep within a mountain forest
    Breezes soft are whispering
Through the dark-robed firs and hemlocks,
    Over Dollie's Spring.

Swiftly glides the tiny streamlet,
    While its laughing waters sing
Sweetest song in all the woodland —
    "I — am — Dollie's Spring!"

Round about, fleet-footed sunbeams,
    In a golden, fairy ring
Dancing, scatter brightness o'er it,
    Pretty Dollie's Spring!

In the dim wood's noontide shadow
    Nod the ferns and glistening
With a thousand diamond dew-drops
    Bend o'er Dollie's Spring.

Shyly, on its mossy border,
    Blue-eyed Dollie, lingering,
Views the sweet face in the crystal
    Depths of Dollie's Spring.

> Years shall come and go, and surely
>   To the little maiden bring
> Trials sore and joys uncounted,
>   While, by Dollie's Spring,
>
> Still the firs shall lift their crosses
>   Heavenward, softly murmuring
> Prayers for her, where'er she wanders —
>   Far from Dollie's Spring.

"Oh, oh, oh!" cried Kittie and Bess together, as Pet concluded, "who is Dollie? which one of us is Dollie?" But Randolph only laughed and wouldn't tell.

With their gay spirits fully restored — for it is as hard for boys and girls to keep solemn as for squirrels to keep from climbing — they told stories, laughed, talked, and raced, all the way home. Supper over, the evening passed swiftly, and bidding uncle Will and aunt Puss good-night, they trooped off to their rooms for the last time. Tom and Randolph were soon asleep, but the girls, I suspect, stayed awake for a good while, talking over the long, sweet summer days that were ended. At last brown eyes and blue were closed. High above, out of all reach of night, but shining down lovingly into it, the stars kept watch over the old farm-house; and He who neither slumbers nor sleeps, held the weary child-world in His arms.

Did our young friends return home safely? Did they see much of each other that winter in Boston? Was Randolph successful in school; and how did they all pass Christmas? There is no room here for answering so many questions; but you can find out all about them in the next number of this series,

"THE NORTHERN CROSS."

www.ingramcontent.com/pod-product-compliance
Lightning Source LLC
Chambersburg PA
CBHW031744230426
43669CB00007B/482